Zebrudaya

This book is a true-life story of Chief Chika Okpala a.k.a Zebrudaya. It is indeed a reflective account of the fascinating life and impactful professional work of Nigeria's foremost comedian and comic actor. His brilliant use of a unique language which he patented and refined, as well as his flair for spontaneous deployment of satire, mark him out as a true legend. His national and international awards/ honours are quite impressive.
But Chika Okpala is not only a comedian extra ordinaire. His portrait is also that of a loving family man. Doubtless, this book will inspire many in and outside the creative, performing and TV broadcasting sector. This book not only shines the light on creativity and family values but also uplifts us with the clear message that we still have great role models, Chika Okpala being one of them.

The book periscopes his formative years, early education, and maturation into adulthood, showing how his parentage, family background and other experiences shaped his emergence as a comedic force and fueled his rise to fame.
Chika Okpala's memories of and reflections on the Nigeria-Biafra war mark his journey into the world of acting during and after the war. The book also touches on James Iroha, the man who conceived the long-running Masquerade series and played a key role in the making of Chief Zebrudaya. The reader will be afforded a glance into the history of Nigeria's film industry and the evolution of Nollywood.

As a first-born in a family of six, Alexander Nkwere Iheke (Opiegbe) plays the role of a bridge to future generations. Passionate to play a role in the preservation of Igbo language, tradition and culture, Iheke is the publisher of Merchants of Success, Igbo Basics for Beginners in America and Mazi Ukonu: Journey from Medicine to Theater Art. Iheke is also publisher of Igbobasics.com and BasicsExpress.com amongst others.
In the aftermath of the Nigeria-Biafra War, citizens had to find a path back to normal life. Comedy arose as a tool to offer solace and

calm people's frayed nerves. Enter Chief Chika Okpala with his storied New Masquerade comedy show. Mazi Ukonu, a celebrated broadcaster, became the bridge between Iheke the author and Okpala the co-author of this book, The Man and Legend of New Masquerade, Chief Zebrudaya Okoroigwe Nwogbo Alias 4:30. This fascinating work will entertain and inform any reader. As Zebrudaya would say, "Ka Chineke mezie okwu.

The Man & Legend of New Masquerade

Chief Zebrudaya

Okoroigwe Nwogbo Alias 4:30

Alexander Nkwere Iheke (opiegbe)
&
Chika Chukwunonso Okpala (Zebrudaya)

Copyright © 2023 by Media Works LLC, Elizabeth, New Jersey USA

All rights reserved. No part of this book may be reproduced in any form including electronic or mechanical means, photocopying, and information storage and retrieval systems, except in the case of brief extracts for the purpose of critical articles and reviews, without permission in writing from Media Works LLC.

Published by Media Works LLC
Elizabeth, New Jersey, 07208 USA

www.mediatworks.com

www.ChiefZebrudaya.com

Book cover design by Alexander Iheke: Chief Chika Okpala a.k.a Chief Zebrudaya during an episode of New Masquerade

Printed in USA. First printing
ISBN 978-0-9844666-2-7 (PBK5.25X8)
ISBN 978-0-9844666-3-4 (hard)
ISBN 978-0-9844666-4-1 (Ebook)
ISBN 978-0-9844666-5-8 (PBK 6X9)

Acknowledgments

I want to thank my coauthor Chief Chika Okpala aka Zebrudaya for trusting me to complete this book and for his draft of the factual materials in this book.
To my late friend Dr. Celey Okogun, CEO of Novel Porter Communications who was the catalyst anchor and driving force in Nigeria for this book project which he christened "Project EY", I am eternally grateful
To Ms. Wanda Williams Master Sgt. Rtd. USA Air Force, who gave unbiased critique on the draft copy of the book to shape its outcome.
Dr. Peter Igho who was the former Executive Director at NTA and Executive Producer of the New Masquerade, who provided the forward to give direction to readers of this book. I value your precision of bringing the New Masquerade to National limelight by recognizing the unique gift of Chika Okpala.
Professor Eme Ekekwe for his encouraging words to do this book thoroughly to befit the larger than life status for the character of Chief Zebrudaya Okoroigwe Nwogbo, Alias 4:30, I remain humbled.
To Barrister Mrs. Anire Okogun, who behind the scenes with her late husband Dr. Celey Okogun, fueled the force to stabilize this project, I am deeply appreciative of your contributions.
Judge and Film maker Oliver Mbamara, for bringing Zebrudaya to New York and New Jersey, which led to the reconnecting that restarted the book writing. Your tremendous impute and participation in this project is treasured.
Brother Paul Uti of NY, provided some basic encouragements during very tough times to ensure that the book project continued. Thank you.
Dr. Uche Anioke, who was Chief ZBs teacher at ESTU, thank you for leading us to other participants in this project. Also many thanks to Okpani Nkama, for his research and impute in concert with Dr. Celey Okogun, on the draft for this book, your participation remains invaluable.

This book gained greatly from the eagle eyes of our readers and book reviewers; Professor Ngozi Ijioma, Professor Okey Ndibe and Rev. Msgr. Anselm I. Nworgu, who crossed the I's and dotted the t's to conclude and bring this book to fruition. I am very grateful.

To members of the Board of trustees for Chika Okpala Foundation for Artistes; Most Rev. Dr. Martin Igwe Uzoukwu, Catholic Bishop of Minna, Dr. Philip UmeEzoke, Dr. Tony Aposhere, aka Zachy, of the New Masquerade, Barrister Vona Igodo standing in for late Dr. Celey Okogun, Chief Clement Ezeh, Rudolf Okonkwo, Host of the Dr. Damages Show and 90 Minuets Africa, and Chief Chika Okpala, Zebrudaya. We are truly appreciative of the stars from Nnobi, Anambra State, Nigeria. Thanks also to Samuel Afeni and the Media Works team for your "photogravision" and interviews of Lizy Ovueme, aka Ovularia, in Port Harcourt and Davis Ofor aka Claurus, in Aba. Your hard work on ground at Zodiac Studios, Abakpa Nike played a good role in this production.
Many thanks to our technical sources; George A. Sanchez at InterBlue Web Union NJ and Donna Loessel at Gregory Press, Kenilworth, NJ USA.

To Governor Alex Oti, the Government and people of Abia State, thank you for honoring alive, Chief Chika Okpala at 75 and thus providing some concluding materials and pictures to highlight, "The Man and Legend of New Masquerade Chief Zebrudaya Okoroigwe Nwogbo alias 4:30".
Truly the Man and Legend of New Masquerade Chief Zebrudaya Okoroigwe Nwogbo alias 4:30 was made possible as a result of Labor of love persistence, unrelenting efforts of the author amidst family hesitation after the publication of the book 'Mazi Ukonu, Journey from Medicine to Theatre Arts. Thank you.
This book is a Legacy Project. I am very grateful for the role each person played to make this book possible. Enjoy the reading of this book, and as Zebrudaya would say, as echoed by Mazi Ukonu, "Ka Chineke mezie okwu" (May God bless the word)

TABLE OF CONTENTS

PART SIX

Nollywood and State of the Nation

6.1 The Nollywood: Challenges & Prospects
6.2 State of The Nation in Perspective

APPENDIX

The New Masquerade Stars At A Glance

1. Chika Okpala - CHIEF ZEBRUDAYA
2. James Iroha - GRINGORY AKABOGU
3. Lizzie Evueme - OVULARIA UREDIA NWOGBO
4. Davis Offor - CLARUS MGBOJIKWE
5. Claude Eke - PRINCE JEGEDE SHOKOYA
6. Christy Essien Igbokwe - AKPENOR
7. Romanus Amuta – NATTY
8. Veronica Njoku – RAMOTA
9. Tony Akposhere – ZACHY
10. Roy De Nani – SERGEANT KPAFU
11. Ifeanyi Gbulie – IKENGA
12. Camilla Mbrekpe – BOMA

FOREWORD

Over the years, millions of Nigerians, who have watched content on their TV screens will acknowledge that Chief Chika Okpala, famously known as Zebrudaya in the evergreen drama series, Masquerade, is easily one of the best actors Nigeria has been blessed with. The spontaneous use of his unique language, his brilliant response to any situation and the numerous awards, fans and friends that he has garnered through many years of bringing joy and laughter through satire, mark him out as a true legend.

Like most Nigerians watching TV before the birth of NTA in 1977, I was a great fan of three notable studio based drama series - Village Head master, Masquerade and Samanja! I particularly was enthralled by the cast of the three series and was ever so anxious to meet them. My secondary education was in Kaduna and I had the opportunity to appear in a few programmes at Radio Kaduna Television – RKTV. I was fortunate to meet the cast of Samanja.

I formally joined the television family in 1975 at the defunct NTV Sokoto; and the following years, my excitement knew no bounds when I finally met the stars of Village Headmaster and Masquerade. I was particularly intrigued by Chika Okpala; a funny and charming young man, who, with makeup (which he applied himself) and sheer brilliant acting, is transformed into an elderly, no-nonsense Zebrudaya! We became friends but I never really could hide my admiration for this great talent!

However, Chika Okpala is much more than an actor. He worked closely with me when I was producing the iconic series, Cock Crow at Dawn. As it was the first drama series shot entirely on location outside NTA studios, many young staff were attached to the production to gain practical experience.

Chika Okpala was one of them. He was always punctual at call times and showed great dedication to whatever assignment he was given which added great value to the production. It is no wonder that when he was assigned the production of Masquerade, he excelled and successfully handled the series for many years.

He is fully committed to his work and never allowed personal problems affect or deter him. I recalled when his daughter was in hospital with what turned out to be a terminal ailment; I went a number of times with him to visit her. He would leave her hospital ward and head back to the studios to record. No one, except possibly me, who knew the great pain in his heart.

He exemplifies the great Nigerian entertainers who put their hearts and souls into their jobs at the expense of their families and loved ones. He seems to reaffirm the saying, "The show must go on!"

This is especially important for Chika, who though committed to his career, is a loving family man. He is also very respectful, never allowing his success to affect his relationships, young and old, friends and colleagues.

In every generation in history, there appears a character very special and unique who stands out and is irreplaceable. Chief Chika Okpala, Zebrudaya Okorigwe Nwogbo, alias 4.30 is one such Nigerian. I am happy and honored to know him and to have worked closely with him.

I am particularly happy too that this great work is coming out to celebrate this great artist. I must commend the creative team and publisher for the tremendous efforts, dedication and meticulous planning to ensure they come up with a worthy product. This book will no doubt be an inspiration to many in and outside the creative, performing and TV broadcasting industry.

In this day and age, when we are inundated with negative news and filled with despair, this book shines the light, not only on creativity, dedication, and family values but also uplifts us with the clear message that we still have great role models and Chika Okpala is one of them!

Dr. Peter Igho (MFR)

OVERVIEW OF THIS BOOK

This book is certainly not a work of fiction. It is a true- life story. Indeed, a reflective account of the life and works of Nigeria's foremost comic actor to rise under the African skies in our time. Welcome to an exciting safari into the world of the famous TV thespian - **Chika Chinonso Okpala; aka Chief Zebrudaya Okoroigwe Nwogbo** alias **4:30**, *Chief His Royal palm wine powerless*. Call him the famous TV masquerade (*Okenmanwu)* of the NTA New Masquerade fame, for his Zeus image on the all-time great satiric drama series.

Who is Chika Okpala? Where did he come from in Nigeria? What was his early education and his growing up like? His family background and parentage, his adult life, work experience and rise to fame. Indeed, his larger than life image presents him akin to the proverbial elephant and the seven blind men in which each described from the area he groped. This is to say, there is always a complex perspective to the lives of great men like Chief Chika Okpala, who stands tall today with a mountain of national and international awards/ honours, including two national honours; **Member of the Order of the Niger** (MON), and **Member of the Federal Republic** (MFR) This is in addition to his global honour as the **UN Rescue Noble Ambassador for Peace in Africa**

To cover the complex perspectives of the life journey of this multitalented mega star, his triumphs and travails, we had to break the story into six parts with subheadings for chapters. Each subheading covers a range of stages in his life journey to date.

ORIGIN

The vision of this book was conceived in 1984-85 after my National Youth Service Corp (NYSC) mandantory one year. The New Masquerade was the biggest show running on NTA Channel 6, Aba in the then Imo State. Mazi Ukonu was the Director General of NTA, Aba, while Chief Sam Mbakwe was Governor of the State. Our company, Trans-Atlantic Concepts Ltd (TAC), a graphic design and advertising company, was based at 90 Faulks Road Corporate Building of Charles Iheke Enterprises Ltd.

Emulating the trending shows and comic magazines of 1980s, such as Lance Spearman, Boom with Fearless Fang episodes and Boomerang, we conceived the idea of **Zebrudaya In Pictures** as a comic magazine in cartoon form laced with actual photographs and combined with cartoon highlights. The idea was finetuned and initial scripts were drafted. The production would combine acts of New Masquerade with practical photo shoots of journey with the fisherman and the boat people of then waterside, Aba. The expedition was to begin from the waterside bridge built by Chief Ugorji Eke, Omefuru onye odiri on rented canoe. In the concept, our destination was to be the source of that Aba River where the production would culminate.

In association with Barrister Okey Uzoho and Chilaka, our cartoonist, the scripting and sketch drawings were develpod. With the kind permission of Mazi Ukonu, we negotiated and agreed with NTA, Aba for the rights to obtain the VHS tapes of all episodes of the New Masquerade from which we were to extract still pictures for the production of **Zebrudaya In Pictures,** a comic magazine.

An Industrial Engineer, Iboko Imo Iboko of 16 Milverton Avenue, accompanied this author to the agreement meeting with Mazi Ukonu at NTA, Ogbor Hill, Aba.

The Federal Government, at the time, had an unenviable record of retiring budding stars, even at the peak of their careers. So it came to be, Mazi Ukonu was unceremoniously retired as General Manager, NTA, Aba. The result of that retirement culminated in jettisoning our dream for the production of **Zebrudaya In Pictures** which was already in motion at the time.

Mr. Okereke who took over from Mazi Ukonu as General Manager, NTA, Aba, literarily took our concept of **Zebrudaya In Pictures** and collaborated with one Moghalu, whose advertising company, SAC was based at Okigwe Road, Aba. It became a case of stolen dreams! Of course, with the connivance of Chilaka, our graphic artist, who eventually left us to work with Moghalu's Company, SAC, they made an expected swine-like end of the stolen dreams. Their failure was monumental as they battled to produce only two (2) editions after much noise and rested the magazine.

The clueless Mr. Okereke wrecked more havoc unrestrained. In his total disregard for record keeping and preservation of historical facts, he committed an even bigger blunder, that saw the VHS library at NTA Aba effectively erased. The library containing the archives of episodes of the New Masquerade was wiped out as they went on to record over the VHS tapes instead of spending to procure new tapes. Thus, for that reason one cannot, today, find many complete episodes of the longest running drama series in the library of NTA Aba.

Dreams rarely die! The idea of documenting Zebrudaya in print was again rekindled in the year 2009-2010 in the most auspicious way. While researching materials to compile the book, *Mazi Ukonu, Journey from Medicine to Theatre Arts,* a commemorative 80th birthday book on Mazi Ukonu, Chief Chika Okpala a.k.a Zebrudaya came into New Jersey, USA to play a leading role in Oliver Mbamara's "Cultures", a comedy series to relive the comedy experience of our growing up years, but this time in far away America.

As destiny will have it, providence provided me the opportunity to meet with Chief Chika Okpala for the very first time in real life at Odabro African Restaurant and Lounge in Orange, New Jersey, USA, owned by Andrew Onyewuenyi. After a brief discussion on the Mazi Ukonu work, Chief Okpala and I, Chief Iheke agreed to an interview with the Publisher of Igbo Basics Publications as part of his contribution to the documentary on Mazi Ukonu, his former Boss at NTA during the heydays.

The interview took place at the home of lawyer/film maker, Oliver Mbamara in New Jersey, USA. The book and documentary DVD was presented at Igbere on March 5, 2010. Mazi Ukonu passed away on January 6, 2020 and was buried on April 2021 at his hometown, Igbere in Bende LGA, Abia State, Nigeria.

I ensured that Chief Chika Okpala, one of the few remaining members of the cast from New Masquerade, attended the burial ceremony of Mazi Ukonu at Igbere. Zebrudaya was welcomed to Igbere by Chief Ukonu Ukonu Jr. (Achi) and guided by Iyke Ekeoma of Igbere who was a former Newscaster at NTA Aba. That trip to Igbere was the event that rekindled the concept of the book on Chief Chika Okpala a.k.a Zebrudaya Okoroigwe Nwogbo Alias 4:30.

That our heroes past and present may never be forgotten even while they are still alive is one of the driving forces for my continued contribution toward the preservation of Igbo language, tradition and culture of which the original dream was supposed to yield. Here we have it. The book that was meant to be, is finally a reality of a dream come true!

Alexander Nkwere Iheke (Opiegbe)

PROLOGUE

It remains a paradox that the television family sit-com that gripped the entire nation, providing post-war comic relief and evening pastime in most homes emerged from the ashes of the catastrophic inferno that was the Nigeria-Biafra War. Indeed, the remote and immediate causes of the war, the resultant gory conditions and effects formed the conception and content of the famous TV drama. As a matter of fact, the development of the plot, the characters, the massaging slanting of **Chief Zebrudaya Okoroiogwe Nwogbo Alias 4.30,** the chief cast, and the entire **New Masquerade** crew, took firm roots in the compelling necessity to provide psychological succour and healing for the surviving populace of the civil war.

Born **Chika Chinonso Okpala,** his father, a successful businessman wanted Chief Zebrudaya to be a banker. For this, he chose to send him to a commercial secondary school instead of the conventional grammar school that was the popular trend then. But this was not to be, for the outbreak of the civil war did not only change this noble parental vision for young Chika, but also his personality and profession forever. At this time, it was a prestigious trend for boys of his age in the Eastern Region of the civil war years to join the Biafran Army. But as fate would have it, this desire did not materialize for young Chika. The more he struggled to join the army, the more the recruiting officers rejected him. Nevertheless, for a determined soul with positive mind like young Chika Okpala, adversities are often turned into modicums for paradigms. He refused to be frustrated into giving up by the humiliating situation, moreso, when his younger sibling was eventually accepted into the Biafran Army. He took to acting and proved a glorious combatant with his drama, entertaining and helping to re-psyche the wounded and traumatized survivors of the battles across Biafra.

Chika garnered accolades for playing this critical role in what was known as *the war efforts* in Biafra without wearing the army uniform, even from the same commander who had twice rejected him from joining the Biafran Army.

He reflected on this twist of fate for him in an interview with the BBC World Service in his characteristic comic language thus;

> *Are you see what I am saw, my play group, Two Cities Play House was proceed to 66 Brigade headquarters Nnobi on their special invite to entertain the officers and men of the brigade. To my surprisation, the same Brigade commander who was refusal to recruit me in the army was praise me to say the play I am do now are also part of my contribute to win the war because why the soldiers are need entertainment to cushion their warfront trauma. If I was in the army would I have does this good play?*

Apparently, like the proverbial rejected stone, Chika's inimitable talent for comics became some soothing balm to the souls and psyche of the embattled Biafra soldiers who survived and returned from the war fronts, unknowingly laying the foundation for a critical aspect of the post-war-resettlement efforts in the land. When the war eventually ended and Chika rushed to Enugu like other survivors, in search of the limited job opportunities from the ruins of the war, providence was again at work to keep him on track of his calling as an actor. He bumped into his former acting mates who had also come from the village to Enugu for greener pastures. It was from here that his destiny with the comic acts and drama got its definition, intertwined with his chance meeting of **Mr. James Iroha,** a producer with Eastern State Broadcasting Service (ESBS).

Mr. Iroha was the creator and scriptwriter of the Masquerade, who later played the role **of** *Gring o ry Akab og u*, in the New Masquerade. From then onwards, a chain of events led young Chika into state performances before the Sole Administrator of the Eastern Region, Mr Ukpabi Asika, Army Generals - Joe N Garuba, TY Danjuma in Kaduna, and finally, the Head of State, Gen. Yakubu Gowon at the State House, (Dodan Baracks) Lagos. The huge success he recorded in these outings prompted young Chika into making the crucial decision of life to devote his entire career to acting and drama. The ultimate results of this decision are all seen in his iconic footprints in the world of acting in Nigeria, Africa and the world at large. One of these iconic footprints lay in the fact that Chika Okpala and his New Masquerade crew, as well as the other television series of the 1970s, 80s and 90s era laid the foundation for Nollywood, the Nigerian film industry, as we know it today.

Now, as you pick up this book to savour, I assure you of a thrilling long walk into the life and works of Chika Chinonso Okpala, Nigeria's, and indeed Africa's foremost TV personality and comic actor, popularly known as **Chief Zebrudaya Okoroigwe Nwogbo alias 4.30.** *"Just go on andjollifikate"*, as he would hilariously say!

Celey Okogun, PhD

A New York Artist impression of Zebrudaya

1987: A Nigerian artist's impression of Chief Chika Okpala

PART ONE

EARLY LIFE & EDUCATION

1.1 His Birth, Siblings & Parentage

1.2 The World and the Nation at His Birth

1.3 His Primary Education & Early Attraction to Movies and Acting

1.4 His Secondary Education

His Birth, Siblings and Parentage

Chief Chika Chukwunonso Okpala [MON, MFR, FTA UN Ambassador]; was born into a typical African polygamous family. His father, **Chief Daniel Nnaike Amanchukwu Okpala,** (*Ezeogomegbunam*) had two wives. Chika was the second son and equally the second child of the ten children from

1963 Lolo Ezinne and her children;
Seated center my loving late mother Gladys Urunwa Okpala, at her right seated my late Senior brother Chief Chike Okpala, standing in front by their legs, right is Nduka Daniel Okpala, left is Chinyere Okpala (both are late) bless their souls. To my mother's far right are Mr Ifeanyi, and Mrs Regina Onachukwu Ezenwanne nee Okpala, at her immediate left standing are Mr Bosa Okpala and my humble self Amb. Chief Chika Okpala Mon mfr fta, UN Rescue Noble Ambassador for peace in Africa. My three other siblings Mr. Eric Azubike, Mr James Obinna, and Mrs Gloria Chioma nee Okpala we're not born then, so they were not in the photograph.

his mother who was his father's first wife.

The second wife, Martha Okpala, who was married into the family a little later, had only one child, a son, making up the nine sons and two daughters his father had.

Above is a group photograph of my family in the 60s

We had two women and they are still alive today. Out of the boys, we have lost three from my mother. My senior brother Chike N.C. Okpala, who was a principal of Government Technical School (GTC) at Awka, Anambra State and was later promoted to a Director of Education in the state. Unfortunately, he died as Director of Education. He died of hypertension.

Chika attested emotionally.

In their order of birth his siblings were; Chike N.C. Okpala (late), who was the first born of the house and was the only one born before Chika (Chief Zebrudaya). Then followed two other brothers Benson Ifeanyi Okpala, a businessman based in Lagos, Nigeria and Bosah Okpala, who is also a businessman based at Nkpor, Anambra state.

It was after these four boys that the first daughter of the house, Regina Okpala, now Regina Ezenwanne, was born to the great joy of the household. She too took to teaching like her elder brother Chike and made a humble mark in her teaching profession, retiring as a Headmistress.

Gloria Chioma Okpala, now Mrs. Obeche, their second daughter and the tenth child of the family from his mother also took to teaching.

Before her were four other sons. Nduka Daniel Okpala (late) was the 5th son of the house and was a businessman based in his hometown, Nnobi. Chinyere Okpala, the 6th son of the house died as a little child. The 7th son, Azubike Eric Okpala is a businessman based in Texas, USA. Obinna James Okpala, the 8th son of the house, is a Business Administration First Class graduate of Enugu State University of Science and Technology (ESUT). Obinna, an Akwa-based businessman, equally holds a

Masters Degree from the same university. Ubaka Ezekiel Okpala, the only son of his stepmother also died as an infant.

Teased that they were only one child short of a football team in the family, Chika stirred mythical laughter enthusing hilariously; "Yes! In fact, they wanted to have thirteen to have Linesmen as well..."

Asked when he was born, day and date, Chika laughed and retorted in his Zebrudaya language;

How I am to know date of birth? "I Am the one who are born myself Ndeh!" I de person who are born myself?

Told me!" "Anyway, let me proceed to tellyou hoha. . . My father and mother told me I was born June 10, 1950. . .Because, I wouldn't know myself when I was born...so,I asked questions and they told me I was born at Ahoada. Ahoada is now in Rivers State.

Ahoada was the divisional Headquarters of so many villages that make up Ekpeye/Engeni County Council

As far as I can remember, Ekpeye/Engeni community is made up of Ahoada, Akpena, Orupata, Edeoha, Abarikpo, Ala-Ahoada, Ojemeni, Iwuogo, Ihubu r uko, Upataabo, and so many small villages, including Joinkarama. After some time, my father thought that I should be brought up at Nnobi, Anambra State and then sent me back home to his mother, my grandmother, Margaret Okpala.

Apparently, Chief Chika Chukwunonso Okpala was born and raised in a core African communal family setting under a strict disciplinarian father who ensured peace and harmony prevailed among his wives and children in his richly blessed preponderance household. Chika's mother and senior wife of the house, Ezinne Gladys Urunwa Okpala who was from Amadunu Ifite, Nnobi, Anambra State and his stepmother,

Martha Okpala also from Nnobi were both seamstresses and they all lived under one roof without any qualms.

> *I grew up to see both my mother, Gladys and stepmother, Martha as seamstresses, each having her own shop-at Ahoada main Market (Ogwumabiri). I grew up to notice there was seriousness in their businesses as they were made to contribute to the feeding of the house. While my mother took charge of soup and stew in our menu, my stepmother took charge of Akpu/ Garri and pounded yam. My father provided rice, beans, meat and fish for the house. I nevernoticed quarrels between my mom and stepmother. Ours was a very peaceful family and this peace subsisted beyond the passage of our three parents . . . The first of the trio to pass on in 1987 was our step mother, Lolo Martha Okpala. My mother, Lolo Ezinne, Gladys Urunwa Okpala, was the last to go twenty-three years later in 2010. This was ten years after the windy exit of our iconic father, Chief Danie Nnaike Amanchukwu Okpala, Ezeogomegbunem, in 1997.*

In a typical African communal setting especially in our clime, when fathers transit, their sons inherit their responsibilities. These include that of ensuring the survival of the family, defense and protection of the family name and heritage etc. The traditional order and hierarchy of authority in the family setting are never in doubt in the event of the transition of fathers. The scepter (ofo) of supreme authority and leadership lies squarely with the Reubens, (diokparas) being the first sons of the House. For the House of Daniel Okpala of Nnobi, the scepter lay with big brother Chike while he lived. Chika's intimidating global image, his beclouding rise to fame and his platinum esteem in public darling-hood notwithstanding.

Nevertheless, it is quite common in Igboland to see more economically capable younger siblings taking over the leading role in their family responsibilities from their elder siblings who may not be as financially fortunate as they were. While this is quite commendable and accepted, it does not, however, take away the Reuben-hood from the less financially capable living elder sibling in the family.

This Igbo aphorism says it all; "Ulu ji ego kwaa Nnaya n'obughi diokpara gburu ya." Meaning; "a more capable second son can take over the funeral rites of their father for the firstborn is not his killer."

Although Chika's silver and gold status could never have matched his priceless name and gargantuan global image, he still proved a worthy younger sibling to his big brother Chike while alive. To his younger siblings, he surely did not let them down as a worthy big brother;

> *I provided financial assistance in their education and trade-apprenticeship. Built common shelter for all of them before some of them set out to their respective inherited landed properties. Up-till date some of them are still in the common shelter*

HIS FATHER

Chief Daniel Nnaike Amamchukwu Okpala Ezeogoegbunam was of the Ifite Ogba-diji clan in Nnobi, Anambra state. He was a shrewd artisan who by sheer hard work, discipline and serious-mindedness made a modest wealth that announced him into reckoning at Nnobi. He was indeed a man of many skills; hence he engaged in different trades and made a huge success of them for a living. He plied as a bicycle repairer, a repairer of basins, pans and cooking pots (tinker) and then progressed from a petty trader of articles (common items of daily need), to a major distributor and sales representative of the Nigeria Tobacco Company (NTC) products in Ahoada, Rivers state before the Nigeria-Biafra War.

Daniel began the rat race of life at Onitsha before migrating to Ahoada, which was a County Council Headquarters' in the old Eastern Region of colonial Nigeria of the 1940s/50s. Nnobi is a couple of kilometers away from Onitsha. It was therefore quite natural that people of the area migrated in numbers to Onitsha in quest of greener pasture before heading elsewhere to sojourn. This was the case with young Daniel Okpala who left Nnobi for Onitsha and later for Ahoada in quest of a means to eke out a living. In his comical ways, Chika described his father's movement in quest of greener pasture thus;

> *'Like other young men, Daniel was leave the lion's den (Nnobi) to proceed to look for greener pasture; what he will be does to get money, to marry wife and get children, and train his children, and to build a home for them and make life easy for them . . . and that are why he was landed himself igidigbam in Ahoada Rivers State via Onitsha"*

Daniel's daybreak to fortune came with his landing the distributorship of Nigeria Tobacco Company products from the UAC sometime in 1958/59. In their marketing drive the UAC sales officers who included a white man were going into villages with urban settings to raise distributors and sales Agents to market their cigarettes. An influx of people from across the country, especially, people of the old Eastern Region into Ahoda, the community was eminently qualified to get a sales outlet established.

UAC officers were said to have gone from shop to shop inspecting and assessing many shops in their quest for a suitable one to select. When they came to Daniel Okpala's shop for assessment, they took cognizance of the size, the way he displayed his articles and other stuffs, the strategic location of the shop and said; *"yeah! We can sell our cigarettes here!"* So, they settled for him to be their main distributor and gave him some bundles and cartons of cigarettes to sell, and after selling he should come to Port Harcourt – their head office to render account. Contrary to the cash and carry buying and selling he was accustomed to, UAC men offered him a rebate deal which he didn't initially understand. According to Chika, his father probably misunderstood the word rebate for rebirth as he was said to have displeasingly queried the officers retorting; *"rebirth! You want to reborn me again?"* They were said to have amusingly and politely told him, No! They were not offering to reborn him, but *to give him rebate* which means, to be supplying him products for sales at discounted rate and be paying him back the excess of his sales periodically after some time. Apparently, his limited education and exposure was an issue here, but he intelligently managed it and averted a truncation of the deal.

Daniel was true to whom he was, a typical Igbo trader, never too frightened of taking business risks and not given to easy fear of sustaining losses or daring the unknown for a business prospect. Gain or lose, life and business must go on. So, he decided to give the new business prospect a chance with the UAC. Indeed, "all things worketh well for the good of those who loveth him." says the Holy Book. Because providence was with Daniel in the venture, even the elements and the environment were equally right and favorable for this breakthrough whose time had come. This manifested in the fact that the Ekpeye people and other peoples of the entire environ were coastal communities and thus inclined to smoking.

O yes! Because they were people by the river, we are call dem water side people or de dem people of Ikpere mmiri, who are suffering sufferty of plenty of cold. So therefore, dey are smoke cigarette nyafunyafu . . . notweeds oo! Cigarettes that are come from de Nigeria Tobacco Company.

Chika stated in his comic language to affirm to the inclination of the people to smoking.

Settling for the deal, young Daniel launched into the sales with all his heart and might. The result and reward of his hard work was instantaneous. In two weeks, he had sold off all the consignments about 50 cartons. So, he ran back to Port Harcourt asking for more. The highly impressed UAC officers gave him 100 cartons and he chartered a vehicle and brought them to his shop at Ahoada. Indeed, nothing stops a blind arrow of success shot right from homing on target. While he was selling and profit was coming, UAC gave him his first rebate after six months, and he couldn't believe what he got. The money was enough for him to build his first house at home – Nnobi. "Are youa!" Are you with me? And that was; *aku ruo uno, okwuo onye kpataraya.*" Meaning; *"when fortune is taken home, it announces who made it."* Hilarious Chika added.

A TOUCHING TESTIMONIAL

In life, it is a common fact that breaking the barriers of success is never without an underlining divine or providential purpose. Chika recounted that when his father got his rebate and made a huge profit, he went home to build his first big bungalow with zinc roof on it. It is worthy of note that at this time in our architectural development, raffia (akirika) and the elephant grass (Atta) were the common and trending roofing materials for houses in Igboland. For his father to roof with zinc means he had arrived and was on top of the world, *"in fact he had arrove!"* He comically added.

It is common knowledge that the pride of success of a son is reveled greatly by his parents. In other words, *a wise son brings honour to his father and pride to his mother*... said King Solomon. This played out here when his father built his two bedroom and parlor bungalow for his aged mother, Lolo Margaret Okpala at home. The mother transmuted into a queen in the esteem of the villagers. Among other things, she became the next provider of free rain water to her fellow wives (Ndi nwunyedi), friends and other women within and outside her compound. They would usually come, with a line up of their clay pots stretching far in the compound. Chika's grandmother's magnanimity was formed by a humiliation she suffered from another family that was the first to build a house with zinc roof in their village.

Chika recalled this ugly experience stating;

According to my father, there was a man who was the big cock crowing in the village. The man later became a titled ICHIE (a revered elder) by name STEPHEN EZEONU, with the title name; ICHIE ONONUGBO.

He had two wives and built a gigantic house, a beautiful house with zinc roof. On this fateful day in the village, there came a sign in the skies that it was going to rain. My grand mother in her agility ran to the compound of Ichie Ononugbo with her own clay pot to be the first to be served if it rained before other villagers came and put in their pots. It wasn't quite thirty minutes or one hour at most when the rain came and filled her pot and the rain stopped. Confidently, and suspecting nothing, she was still in her house relaxed while others were going to check and carry their pots away. By the time she came back to carry her pot, one of the wives of the Ichie had used a machete to smack open and destroy the pot. She could not control her tears especia l y, as she didn' t just go there as a trespasser. The woman's husband, Ichie Ononugbo, in his magnanimity had declared to the villagers to always come and take water any time it rained and went back to Onitsha where he lived. There was no one to report to or did anyone care to console her. The woman's grouse was why should a visitor come and have water in her own compound and from her own zinc before her. My grandmother wept bitterly and went home heart broken without her pot of water. As fate would have it, just as she was entering her compound, lo and behold her son,Daniel riding home with his bicycle.

In those days, they rode bicycle from Ahoada, through Elele into Owerri crossing Ihiala and so many other communities to arrive Nnobi. There was no other means of transport, you couldn't find vehicle, if you did find vehicle at all, you may not afford it. The fare was about three pence, but where do you get three pence? It's Just like people talking about air travels these days, 'shouting they cannot afford it. In those days it was like that, even with the penny-penny, two–two pence that was paid for transport then. On hearing what happened to his other, my father couldn't understand it and was so angry. It was quite devastating that he rode hundreds of miles to come home from Ahoada only to meet his mother weeping that they broke her pot at Ichie Onougbo's house where she went to fetch water. He was said to have knelt down and prayed to God and said; "God please, don't let this repeat itself, give me opportunity to put up a zinc house for my mother."

For this, when the first rebate money he got from the UAC came, he ploughed it all into the building of the house in the village for the mother. "He didn't even think of our welfare, all he thought was how he was to put up a zinc house for his mother in the village. Nevertheless, Chika's father continued to work hard with his sales of the NTC cigarettes and was making money. He was soon to diversify, branching into oil and gas, selling petrol, diesel and kerosene from that same spot. Sadly, his thriving business began to dwindle. He decided to relocate to Azumini in Ukwa, in present day Abia state, and learnt how to patch tanks, broken pots, aluminum pans, basins, etc. He again excelled as a tinker as they were called then), to the point that talks in town were that Daniel Okpala was now an engineer of broken pots.

> *Are you are!" Daniel Okpala are become an engineer. He was engineer of broken pots and pans, provided chop money are proceed from the business.*

Chika joked and continued on a serious note;

> *When you come to his shop there would be hundreds of broken things piled up for him to fix and he charged very minimally, two-two pence,*

> *four-four pence, and five pence to put those stuffs back into use. But that didn't give him as much money as the tobacco company deals.*

Before he went into the tinker trade, it's important to remember that earlier in his days at Ahoada, he had learnt how to repair bicycles. As a matter of fact, that was actually the trade that took him to Ahoada. He had lived and apprenticed with the man he learnt the trade from, but began to realize that the golden fleece he was looking for, did not exist in the bicycle repairing trade. He smartly left the business to engage in his petty article selling business that opened the door for his life and level changing UAC distributorship.

When eventually Daniel returned to Onitsha from Ahoada, many years after he left in the 1940s as a starry-eyed lad desirous of making a meaningful living in his life, he came back a full-fledged family man and a more matured man than when he left the bustling city. He joined his in-law and they shared one large shop in the Onitsha main market, rated the largest market in West Africa then. They both sold textiles.

1.2 THE WORLD & THE NATION AT HIS BIRTH

The year 1950, when Chika Chukwunonso Okpala was born, could be described as the mid rib of the 20th century AD. The world had just broken into the end of the first half and the beginning of the second half of the politically volatile century that witnessed two global military conflagrations in the first half of the century. These were the first and second World Wars fought between 1914 – 1918 and 1939 – 1945 respectively. These wars substantially threatened survival of world nations and indeed, continued existence of mankind upon the face of the earth. This was essentially because of something more fundamental that actually watered the wars and defined the face of the 20th century. These were the gargantuan exploits and advancement made by men of science and technology of that generation.

It is indeed, the ugly side of these earth-shaking advances in science and technology of the 20th century that watered the apocalyptic dimensions of the World Wars with the inventions of the atom bombs, supersonic war machine that fly in air, move on land, and other magnificent war instruments of mass destructions of life. This triggered the infamous nuclear race in which the mega powers of the Eastern and Western blocs of world nations, in a cold rivalry for supremacy of economic and political powers, engaged in inordinate production and acquisition of these killer weapons of mass annihilation in sheer manifestation of man's primordial inclination to evil.

It is pertinent to note also that 50 years earlier in 1950, young Chika Okpala was being born in Nigeria; when Winston Churchill, the all-time great British Prime Minister was declared *Person of the Half Century by American TIME Magazine.* This was for his inimitable statesmanship and the galvanizing role he played to ensure world powers closed ranks and fight to defeat villainous Adolph Hitler of Germany and his ilk of totalitarian ideologues.

Two years before, in 1948, Joseph Stalin who led the Soviet Union into the victorious allied forces to fight the Germans, pulled away from the Allied Nations to continue with his totalitarian communist ideology. He influenced the spread of the decrepit ideology across nations of Eastern Europe forming them into the Eastern bloc nicknamed the *iron curtain.* This triggered further polarization of the world powers into the cold war that dominated the last half of the 20th century, with America and Britain on the lead of the Western bloc.

AFRICA

During these years, Africa was essentially a continental colony shared among the warring European nations in the Berlin Conference of 1885 in Germany. The World Wars were equally fought in Africa, with Africans soldiers deployed in various theatres of the war in Europe, Asia and Africa. Some notable theatres of the World War II in Africa were; Libya**,** Cameroon, Ethiopia, and Somaliland. On the west coast of Africa, the war extended to Liberia and Togo. The British who were at the behest of the World Wars surely exploited their African and Asian colonies to the fullest for the war efforts. These exploitations may have sparked the agitations for liberation from colonial bondage, which began at the end of the World War II.

While Nigeria, Chika Okpala's home country did not experience the shootout and echoes of the big guns of the two world wars; the effects were quite significant, reflecting in the temperament of the British Colonial Authorities of the time. Sir Arthur Richard, who became Nigeria's Governor General in 1943, two years before World War II ended, manifested this with his haughty, no-nonsense attitude, inclined to racism. As an apostle of Churchill, who proclaimed in 1942, he did not become Prime Minister, *"to preside over the liquidation of the British Empire. . ."* which then controlled a quarter of the globe's land, Governor Richard resisted decolonization by blocking inclusion of Nigerians in his Government, even at the Local Council level.

This deepened the nationalist agitation occasioning the longest ever-organized general strike action in colonial Nigeria by African Civil Service Technical Workers Union led by Comrade Michael Imoudu in 1945.

Unyielding, Richard went ahead to enact his infamous 1946 Constitution which Nigerian Nationalists repudiated and dubbed Richard's Imperial Order in Council. This came into force on January 1, 1947 and essentially legitimized Richard's totalitarian racist policies of exclusion of the indigenous population in his administration. This is not withstanding the fact that, as far back as the beginning of the making of Nigeria in 1914 with the Amalgamation by Lord Fredrick Lugard, the country was divided into 21 large Provinces in addition to the Lagos colony.

Northern Nigeria had 11 of the Provinces leaving the South and Lagos with 10 Provinces. Later, the ten Provinces of Southern Nigeria were constituted into Eastern and Western Regions. Out of these ten provinces of the south, Igboland got two and shared the third with Ogoja in Northern Cross River of today.

However, the jinx of non-inclusion of indigenes in governance by the Arthur Richard's government was broken in the Eastern Region; significantly, in the same 1950 Chika was born. It came with the proclamation of the Eastern Region Local Government Ordinance No. 16 of 1950, approved by Sir John MacPherson, who took over from the controversial Richard in 1948 as Nigeria's 5th Governor General since Lugard. It is equally pertinent to point out here that, in the 1950s, when Chika was born, Nigeria was just ten years away from Independence, and had entered the crucial last lap in the struggle for political Independence, which eventually came October 1, 1960. Young Chika, possibly, celebrated the Independence Day with his parents at Ahoada, his place of birth.

AHOADA AT HIS BIRTH

Now, zeroing in on the Ahoada world at the birth of Chika, we must remember that Ahoda and Degema were part of the Owerri Province at the time. Therefore, whatever mutations and reforms that were taking place within the communities under the province were also happening to Ahoada and Degema. Just as the principal communities in the Owerri Province were transforming into Divisional and County Council headquarters, so were Ahoda and Degema.

As Divisional Headquarter, many villages that make up Ekpeye/Engeni County Council were under Ahoada. These include Ahoada, Akpena, Orupata Edeoha, Abarikpo, Ala-Ahoada, Ojemeni, Iwuogo, ihuburuko, Upataabo and Joinkarama. One great feature of Ahoada is her famous Ogwumabiri Market. It is a weekly market that runs every eight days which attracted people from far and near, especially people of the neighboring communities such as Ikwere, Etche, Engeni, Joinkarama, Mbiama, Abua, Okaki, Edagweri, Isua and Osusu. They are people of mixed occupational culture, essentially, farming and fishing. They have cassava farms, plantain and banana plantations as well as palm plantations. They have so many creeks and streams from which they fish for their living.

Just as it is common in Rivers and Ijaw communities, Ahoada and all its neighboring communities engage in annual traditional wrestling contests. The festive wrestling contests is called, *Egelege*. Trophies are won in various categories. They also celebrate *Ojuju* (Mmanwu) Festival where each community showcases various dances and masquerades. Unlike what happens in core Igbo communities, women are not exempted; they take active part in the Ojuju festival.

The people of Ahoada are predominantly Christians belonging to different Christian sects; there are Roman Catholic faithfuls, Seventh Day Adventists, Anglican Communion members, Baptist Church adherents and others. This is by no means ignoring the fact that, in a typical core African society as Ahoada, you must find in their numbers traditionalists and custodians of their culture who hold tenaciously onto their ancestral belief and religion.

It is equally a common fact that loving parents desire seeing their children advance beyond their own limits in life, hence they do all they can to see them go through schools. Chief Daniel Okpala was manifestly one of such parents. In some cases, these noble wishes and parental dreams are stifled by sheer economic incapacity of these parents. Chika Chukwunonso Okpala and siblings were lucky for having a financially and economically capable father who provided for their education and other benefits of life in their childhood.

While their father did not advance beyond Standard II in his education, it was his innate desire to see them, advance to universities and become leading professionals in their careers. He even had clear idea of what he wanted them to become. In the case of Chika, his stubborn second son, that he wanted to become a bank manager, he chose that Chika must go through a Secondary Commercial School instead of the conventional grammar School his first son, Chike passed through. Chief Daniel Okpala provided so well for his children that they could be said to have been born with "silver, if not golden spoon" But hilarious Chika retorted

"Enh! Who are born of silver My father was not produce spoons and forks, he was just tinker of basins! And pots..." Which gold? Nevertheless! Eku! Are you know what are called Eku?

Are you are! Eku are wooden spoon. If I am born with silver or gold spoon, you will not see me here. Are you see what I am saw!"

He enthused triumphantly.

In all climes, civilized or not, life actually begins with the informal education for the individual from home. The micro family unit is the cradle of the lifelong education, socialization and integration of the human person into the society from infancy. Chika passed through this, not only with his parents, but partly with his grandmother in his home town, Nnobi. His father routinely sent him home from Ahoada to his grandmother that he may not forget his root and nativity. This was a common practice with the peripatetic Igbos, especially in those days. It was while he was at home that his journey to formal education began.

This started at St Paul's Primary School, Ebenesi, Nnobi, where he did his (otakara) kindergarten, Primary One and Two up to Standard I.

When a child is about three years he gets into Otakara. This is to say, from 1950 when I was born, to my Otakara, should be 1953 or there about. Then from 1954 to 1956, I was in my ABC reading;

aa bu gb ch d e fg hh.

He said, sniggering at his hilarious recitation of the Igbo alphabets.

He continued

In Standard I, my father said no and recalled me to Ahoada saying he wanted a change of environment better than what I had at Nnobi for me. My senior brother, Chike also read at CMS Central School, Nnobi before he left for Ahoada to join my father. From there he joined one school there in Ikwere, he schooled in Ikwereland.

AKARA ONE SHILLING

My parents lived in Ahoeda; that's where we were born. When we go home on holidays to Ahoeda and want to go back to Nnobi after visiting my parents, since we were staying with grandma while attending school, our parents gave us pocket money like five kobo, ten kobo. We would collect from several sources; plus, the money our mother gave us. So we had money, but what were we going to do with it? So when we get home, as small boys, what do we do with the money? We go and buy akara.

In one of those days, my younger brother and I went and bought akara. We had the money; so we used one shilling. That's a lot of money in those days, but we didn't know.

The mama akara woman asked us where we will put the akara? We took our book bags and threw away our exercise books. We used our book bag to load the akara and went to school.

When it was time for us to submit our homework, we opened our bag and lo it was full of akara.

The teacher was so offended by the smell of akara then he asked, who gave you the money to go and buy akara? Who sold this quantity of akara to you? How much money did you use in buying the akara. I said, one shilling.

After school the students wanted akara. Do you know I was going to go back to the woman who sold the akara to us and she confirmed it was one-shilling worth of akara. She did not ask us what we will do with the akara, all she wanted was to get paid.

They marched us home to my grandmother. We were afraid the consequences would be that nobody would give us money again like they used to.

Back to Ahoeda.

When young Chika returned to Ahoada in 1961, his father enrolled him in Government Primary School, Ahoada to continue in Primary Two. A year after, his father angrily took him out of the Government Primary School, Ahoada, to another primary school in a remote place called Joinkarama in 1962. Why would his father do that? Chika said;

> *He sentenced me to Joinkarama in Engeni. Engeni is part of Ekpeye and Ekpeye is part of Ahoada on your way to a place called Mbiama by the Urashi River, which is a large River that took pontoons and other ferries . That was just for my stubbornness and to remove me from my friends and my mother whom he felt was covering me especially after*

an incident I will tell you shortly. Nevertheless, I did my Standard II to VI in Joinkarama.

HIS EARLY ATTRACTION TO MOVIES

His childhood fantasy was beginning to irk his father who saw such fickle attractions as getting in the way of his studies and his fatherly vision for him. While in Government Primary School Ahoada, he made friends, three of whom, were very close and dear to him. They were **Owen, Femi,** and **Okoroba.** They were all in the same class in Standard IV. Like Birds of same feather, that flocked together, they had this obsession for film shows. Chika recalled;

In those days. there was this Faraday films that came from Port Harcourt to rural villages to show films.

In Ahoada, they came every Friday or Saturday to show these films at the Government Primary School field, Ahoada. On Fridays after school, some of us who behaved in a way that showed we were not Ekpeye boys, but from Onitsha side, were engaged to make a fence to cordon off the field from free passage with only one entrance for them to take their gate fees. Somehow, these film promoters were so stingy and exploitative that they never gave us free tickets to come and watch the films. For this, the four of us planned a way to be gaining entrance to watch the films free of charge. What was in vogue in the townships then was the bucket system toilet. So, while making the fence, we ensured the edges of the fence ended at the back wall by the toilet, thus leaving the bucket-hole of the toilet open. So, when the film show will be on in full capacity, we will remove the empty bucket and crawled into the film arena and watched the films. In the morning at school, four of us will be the ones to tell the story of each of the films we watched to the entire boys.
We equally engaged them with stories we read from some action pictorial

entertainment publications such as the Lance Spear-man and Zuluman Magazines. So, they depended on us to know what the films were.

Chika admitted he was really obsessed with the films and tried to follow what was going on; "especially the cowboy films . . . the way the actors moved, kpoi! Kpoi! Kpoi!, shooting guns, and the way they jumped unto their horses were very entertaining and it engaged us. So, we will tell the rest of the class, those who couldn't come out to watch the films the story of what happened on Friday night."

Asked who was his favourite actor in those early Cowboy films he watched, he mirthfully enthused;

oooh! Jooohn Wayne! As a matter of fact, I must confess that after watching those films, my dream was to become a great actor like John Wayne in the Cowboy films. We heard that Actors overseas were well respected and very wealthy. So, as a boy, my dream was to become a great actor and a film star like John Wayne.

His habit of disturbing the entire yard with his stories of the film he watched became a bother to his father so much that he constantly chastised him saying; "Instead of going to study your books you are going to watch films! Is that why you came to Ahoada? I brought you from the village to town so that you can go into college and come back either a medical Doctor or an Accountant, or a Banker or an Engineer. . . that's why I brought you!" The old man would bellow, biting his finger in livid anger and scorn.This film watching thing really bothered Chika's father to the point that he was just waiting for an auspicious moment to yank him out of the government Primary School, Ahoada, to Baptist Day School, Joinkarama That moment came with this incident;

Yes! One Friday evening, we had set the whole place and as usual marked out where we used to make our free entrance into the film show to watch John

Wayne. And the first boy, Owen, went in successfully, and surveyed the place and signaled us to come in that the road was clear. So, just as the second boy, Okoroba, put his head into the hole, unknown to us, a woman had come to poo-poo . . . All we began to hear was;

para-para-para–pata-pata-pata on the boy's head. One wouldn't know if the woman was purging or what? So, as he panicked and forcefully retreated, the nails on the mouth of the opening caught him on the head and blood gushed from his head. The sight of the gushing blood made us run away, everyone to his father's house, abandoning him to his fate. I ran home and luckily, my father was not yet back home at the time, but he was on his way. So, I came in and dived under the bed and started snoring.

Then it wasn't too long the parents of the boy, Okoroba, took him by hand and brought him. The boy was still bleeding profusely. But what they had done was to wash off the shit (feaces) on his head. So, as they came banging at our door shouting; Chief Daniel . . . Chief Daniel Onaya? (Is Ch i e f Da n i e l h o me?) My heart cut from under the bed I was hiding. They were shouting in Igbo "Una ahula nwa Daniel . . . ike ya egbula nwamoo!" (Look at Daniel's son, he will kill my son). So, my father opened the door and they pushed the boy to him and said; "lookam make una go chopam . . . una don killam . . . see the blood wey dey komot!" My father pleaded with them to allow him to take the boy to the near by Chemist shop where they will treat him.

They had Chemist shops in those days, they didn't have pharmacy. So, they agreed to allow him treat the boy.

Before then my father dragged me out from under the bed with his koboko and finished me. In his rage as he whipped me he yelled; "I brought you out of the village to come here and see the light, but you want to put me into trouble, I will not allow you to put me in any trouble . . . " he gave it to me. My mother tried to come to my rescue and he bawled at her; "if you come near me I will give it to you too." So, when the whipping and my weeping were over,

I followed my father to the chemist shop where they treated the boy. You can imagine me following my father, the kind of tension I had . . so much tension. After treating him, they took him home and we came back to the parlor because we lived in one room and parlor apartment. The one room was for him and his two wives. The parlor was for all the generation and poultry of his children (laughter) plus the housemaid and those learning how to sow, for my mother was a seamstress. So they came around and stayed with us in the house. Seven of us in the house apart from my senior brother who was not there and others who were not born, all of us would lie on the floor with mat.
But I will prefer to go under the bed, the parlor bed. Usually there's a parlor bed by the formation of the houses in those days. In the morning of the next day, my father still unhappy said to me; 'because of you I have not gone to Port Harcourt.

Now, get ready when I come back you will no longer be in Ahoada. I know where you will be. ' He had a friend from Joinkarama, a driver of the Baptist Hospital, Joinkarama. Baptist Hospital was run by Americans and the Chief Medical Director was an American, the nursing Sister was an American and they had all those American people with them there. He (my father's friend) Mr. Miller Amidu, retired military personnel, was their driver and he was a native of Joinkrama. He was also a disciplinarian. Once it was six o'clock in the evening, you are in the house. May be, my father must have briefed him very well to watch this boy, if there's entertainment anywhere he will sneak out. So, I lived with him and all my liberty was cut off. I wasn't going out anymore. I humbled myself, read my books and went to school first thing in the morning. I was also looking after his son; they had only one son, Adokie Miller. So, it was equally my duty to take the boy along with me to school and the school was about a mile away from where we lived. We trek it every morning, and had to leave early to meet up. While Adokie went to the elementary side, I'll go to the standard side. So, that was how I was cut off from my friends and film shows, especially, John Wayne Films… I therefore faced my studies and my houseboy work until 1964, when I gained admission to Prince Memorial High School, Onitsha, then known as Prince Secondary Commercial School Onitsha; Honestly, I cannot tell about the where abouts or what became of my friends Owen, Okoroba and Femi since then till date.

1.4 HIS SECONDARY EDUCATION

Life is indeed a checkered adventure, replete with lights and shades. The hills and valleys, the plains and troughs, we encounter dailydefine the shape and quality of our lives. Sometimes, these experiences may leave us irredeemably battered and shattered psychologically or physically or even both. Some strong willed, like Chika Okpala, adapt and survive as he did with the houseboy challenge in the house of the Millers in Joinkarama. This is another way of saying that those with positive hearts and minds are the toughies that survive the tough times better. No wonder Dr. Robert Schuler opined that; *"tough times don't last . . . (for) when the going gets tough the tough gets going."*

It was obvious that the intention of Chika's father was to cut his son off from his friends, banished him from the lure of film shows as well as dissuade his early fantasies of becoming a John Wayne. It is unclear whether this action proved successful in Chika's advance from primary to secondary school. What is, however, certain is that he had a successful primary education and an equally successful secondary education with flying colours. Don't forget that his father had his own dream career for him. He wanted him to be a banker period! This formed the choice of school and subjects of study.

From his testimonial above, his journey into secondary education began in 1964. After his Standard Six at the Baptist Day School, Joinkarama, he took the entrance examinmation that same year to Baptist High School, Port Harcourt. There was another Secondary School in Port Harcourt. He also took the entrance examination and passed. And then, the entrance examination of Prince Secondary Commercial School, Onitsha which was his father's choice for him. Chika did not know how his father got the contact address of the school. He brought the form to him to fill and insisted that was the school he must attend. He took and passed the entrance examination to that school as well; making it three secondary school entrance examinations he passed that year.

Chika's choice was Baptist High School Port Harcourt, but his father said; *"no, you are not going there, you are going to be a banker, you will need to do Commercial subjects, that's wh a t I i n t e n d fo r y o u . I am a trader ; I want somebody to keep my money for me. "* The father's intention was quite noble and agreeable to Chika. Besides, his mother had earlier advised her son not to disobey his father if he wanted to go further in his education. When it was time to go to Onitsha, Chief Daniel personally took Chika to the Prince Commercial Secondary School. Luckily, the proprietor of the school was from Nnobi, Prince L.N. Okoli. He said to the Principal; "please, this is my son, he is your own, I want him to school here under your watch", he pleaded.

"I think he felt good and satisfied that he was handing me over to to the care and custody of his own person. So, I went there and started schooling." Chika further recalled that while he was being handed over to his school Principal, little did he know his father was also planning to stage a comeback to his abondaned textile trading business at Onitsha. He thought that this was probably for his father to be policing him and finding out whether he had actually stopped going to the movies.

He said his father invited him one day to visit his shop which he was sharing with his in-law at the Main Market Onitsha. He went there and liked what he saw. He could only go there on free days, as every Saturday was not a free day in the school. One day, during one of the holidays, he visited his father's shop; he was amazed at the diverse nationalities of the customers and how his father managed to cope in communicating with them. At the time, Onitsha main market used to host people from all West African countries even up to

South Africa and they spoke French, Portuguese, English, German etc.

JOINING THE DRAMA SOCIETY

In the schools in those days, there were so many social societies open to students to belong and participate in their activities. Popular among these societies, also found in his school, were the school's Debate, Drama, Social, and Literary Societies. Chika's innate interest in films and acting naturally drove him into choosing to belong to the school's drama society. His first participation in a stage drama show in the school was the adaptation of *Man of Character by Ola Rotimi.* He played the role of Bodunde, the son of Man of Character, who also doubled as house help. He refused to accept an offer of a tempting bribe from a jobseeker (fresh from secondary school) who was looking for a job in his father's office. In the story, the father had a very viable company he was running, and this young boy who passed out very well from Secondary School was desperately seeking to be employed in this company, but there were no vacancies.

There was nothing they could do for the boy, his father, the CEO of the company had declared. Desperate as he was, the boy went back and tried all he could including offer of tempting amount of money to get him to talk and influence his father to give him the job. He refused to be compromised saying he could not disobey his father.

Hilariously, Chika said;

> *The one I disobeyed my father in real life landed me in Joinkrama (Laughter)...That was the first play I acted and that first play gave us (the Drama Society), the first prize and I won the Advance Learners Dictionary as the best performer, for my role in the show. And I said an Award of a whole Dictionary we used to*

buy 15 shillings. It was more expensive than any other text book. The second year, we won two consecutive times. And we won again in 1966, the year the military men struck with the first coup in the land that altered fundamentally the run of events and history of this land, Nigeria.

His name was Brown Ezeugwu. Brown took him to their store where they previewed films. And they previewed films they will show through the week until the next Saturday when they will visit again. While they were previewing these films, Chika and his friend had the privilege to see so many interesting cowboy films. Excitedly, he said to himself;

Ah-ah!" Are these not the films my father said I should not watch, the films that made him banish me to Joinkarama in my primary school? Chaee! God I thank you o!

Before now, Chika confessed he had actually lost interest in film shows until he chanced into the opportunity again in Mr. Brown's house which rekindled his interest again in films and acting. Although, he began to like films once more, but it was not as much as before when he dared all odds to go and watch. Besides, there were so many assignments in secondary school that held him down.

However, there was something striking and significant that fundamentally defined his bias towards comedy instead of his earlier interest in the thriller, violent aspects of the John Wayne cowboy films. Chika noted that his interest was being drawn more and more to the 2-3 minutes comedy sketches that heralded the main films as curtain raisers. The effect of these comic teasers was so strong on him that it eventually informed his tilting towards comedy shows.

When the indomitable Drama Society went ahead to win the overall best performers of the school again for the third time in 1967, the Drama Society elected Chika their president. It was a tragic year that denied him the opportunity to exhibit his leadership potential within the Drama Society in the school. The ripples and echoes of the drumbeat of national catastrophe that trailed the two successive coups of January and July, 1966 occasioned the bloody rhapsody of violence that culminated in the bloody Nigeria-Biafra War that raged in the land from July 6, 1967–January 15, 1970.

Just before we get to his reflections on the war, Chika recalled one memorable incident in his secondary school days he will never forget. According to him, Fridays was confession days for all catholic students in the school. So, at 3 pm, all catholics in the school will assemble in the school's assembly hall and Arch Bishop Hirrey of Holy Trinity Catholic church, Onitsha would send Reverend Father Frog Bench to take them in catechism and confession. The students will file out and go one after the other to confess their sins. In the course, Rev. Fr. Frog Bench will request each confessing student to summarise by singing a chorus to signify he was done with his confession. Chika recalled that most students preferred to do the confession in English and sing in Igbo language essentially because Rev. Fr. Frog Bench was a Briton.

On this very occasion, the first student went into the confession cubicle and started;

> *Oh God! Pardon me my sins! I know I have said so many sinful things by word of mouth and by deed. I was born into sin. But I have resolved that from today, henceforth I, Benjamin, by the grace of God Almighty, I will not sin again. Oh God! Please, forgive me my sins in Jesus name! Then he followed up with this popular gospel chorus; My Lord! My God! How excellent is your name! My Lord Jesus how excellent is you now!*
>
> *Then the Rev. Fr. Frog Bench, in absolution of his sins, will respond in Latin;* **Etserede... Etsecredo... Etsecrede!** He will snap his finger saying; "next!", thus dismissing the student.
>
> *The next student will go into the cubicle and repeat; "Oh God please pardon me my sins I know I have said so many sinful things by word of mouth and by deed. I was born into sin. But I have resolved that from henceforth I, William Ufo by your powerful grace I will not sin*

again...Please good Gracious God forgive me my sin in Jesus name! In absolution, Rev. Fr. Frog Bench responded as usual in his Latin; Ets e re d e… Ets e c re d o… Ets e c re d e! The third boy went in shivering, apparently afraid of the white Rev. Fr. He was able to recite the confession statement to a point and suddenly went blank. The Priest waited for few minutes for him to sing his own end of confession chorus and nothing came. Rev. Fr. Bench said to him "I did not hear; "oh God forgive me my sins in Jesus name." Not minding, the Priest, however, urged him to sing. The boy was silent, as he could not remember any song to sing; even to repeat the ones his colleagues sang. An uneasy pause ensued; there was stalemate for few minutes. Then all of a sudden, the obviously jittery boy, burst out in Igbo singing; "Fath e r Fro g B e n c h Lee . . . e m e lam m i njo! Su tue m u w e! Le zu e m a ny a ah u! Ig a am ata n a e m e lam n jo m a b ia m a c o nfe s s io n!" Translated in English; "Lo o k, Fath e r Fro g B e n c h! I have sinned! Rent my clothes and look me over, you will see that truly I committed sin and came for confession!" The spontaneous outburst of laughter by a whole class of about 30 students thoroughly embarrassed the British Priest.

It was it this time that an equally amused indigenous Priest, who was standing by the window observing the confession saved the situation. He not only thoroughly berated the boy for his outlandish performance, but the entire class for laughing stupidly. He narrated that the embarrassing situation of Fr. Bench is what our own Priests and Deacons, sent on missionary work to other country equally faced on account of not understanding the native dialects the indigenes used in making their confessions. He made us understand that Nigerian priests sent to these other lands in Africa, especially in the East African countries such as Zimbabwe, Rwanda etc were assessed on language appreciation and thus expected to understand the native dialects and languages in which they made their confessions.

PART TWO

THE CIVIL WAR AND HIS JOURNEY INTO ACTING

Chapter 2

MEMORIES & REFLECTIONS ON THE CIVIL WAR

The civil war, like the World Wars, defined the face of Nigeria in the last century since creation in 1914. In pre-independence Nigeria, long before Chika Okpala was born, there were tragic crises that rocked this country. There were spates of pacification battles waged against the Nigerian natives by the British colonialists during the years of the World War I.

This was essentially to bring this community coercively constituted into the 21 Provinces of the Southern and Northern Protectorates of Nigeria under their command and control with their direct and indirect rule systems. These conflicts were more in the Southern communities east of the Niger because, they resisted or shunned the Warrant Chiefs' authorities in their domains. The first of these historic crises that rocked the entire Eastern Province was the **Aba Women Riot of 1929.** The crux of the matter was an attempt to include women in the 1929 controversial taxation policy in which Warrant Chiefs of the communities were used as collection agents by the colonial authorities. Though the women vowed to resist any such draconian law aimed at taxing women, the colonial authorities ignored the warning and went ahead with the planned taxation policy. An attempt at enumeration of household for tax purposes at Oloko community snowballed into the historic Aba women riot of 1929.

The other headline crises that engulfed the nation at the time were the 1945 general strike action of workers that paralyzed government for months, the coal miner's tragedy in which 21 miners were shot and killed in cold blood by the colonial police officers in Enugu, and the Tiv riots of 1953 and 1964 against political domination.

On Nigeria's attainment of political Independence in October 1960, more crises threatened her survival as a nation.

A series of pre-and post-independenece crisis deepened the polarization of the country along the eternalized primordial North and South political divide.

It was this ugly picture of a nation engulfed in political anarchy that drew the ire of the military men led by Major Patrick Kaduna Nzeogwu to strike in the early hours of January 15, 1966. Unfortunately, the military interregnum ironically opened another vista of anarchy upon the land with the July 29, 1966 counter coup. General Aguiyi Ironsi and his host, Col. Adekunle Fajuyi were killed in the counter mutiny.

In this deeply fractured nation, vociferous echoes of the people's call for cessation of the Eastern Region from the Federation of Nigeria reverberated across the country and beyond. However, there was a brotherly hand of hope for a political solution to the crisis from Ghana that needed to be exploited. This head of State, Lt. Gen. Joseph Ankrah, barely a year in power, convened the Aburi parley for the warring parties.Though both parties managed to reach an agreement known as the famous **Aburi Accord**, the ink had hardly dried when the agreement fell apart.

On May, 27, 1967, an enlarged Consultative Assembly and the Advisory Committee of Chiefs and Elders of the East rose from a two-day meeting to hand down the mandate of secession to Lt. Col. Odumegwu Ojukwu to declare Eastern Region a republic under the name and title, *The Republic of Biafra*, at the earliest possible date. Governor Ojukwu dutifully carried out this mandate of the people on the 30th day of May 1967. On the same May 30, in a swift response, the Head of State of Nigeria, Gen. Yakubu Gowon promptly renounced the Republic of Biafra and declared it *"a rebellion"* which will be met with a police action by the Federal Military Authorities. On July 06, 1967, a full scale civil war began between Eastern Region, now Republic of Biafra, and the Federal Army.

2.2 JOINING THE WAR WITH DRAMA

Chika Chukwunonso Okpala, had just turned 17 in 1967, when the war broke out. The year was indeed, a very bad year, not just for him, but to all Nigerians, especially, the entire people of the Eastern Region. On a personal note, schools were closed in the Eastern Region, pupils and students sent back to their parents and Guardians. Chika headed home to Nnobi.

Even if Chief Daniel Okpala and family had wanted to stay on at Ahoada during this period, surely there was no guarantee of the safety of their lives and business. So, his early relocation of his business to Onitsha and the buildings he put up at home long before the outbreak of the crisis were both providential and proactive. So, as the crisis deepened by the day with continued influx of surviving easterners from the North, West and elsewhere across Nigeria, many began to relocate down to their communities for safety and security of their homesteads and to provide succour to their surviving returnee relatives.

This influx posed as much a serious challenge to the Government of the East as it was equally to communities. Many who left their jobs, including hundreds of University graduates of Eastern origin and ran home for safety could not find job replacements. Across the communities, tension was rife. The prospect of war loomed large, becoming a more popular option for freedom for the people given the circumstances.

At this point, joining the military service of the Eastern Region became both popular and viable, especially the youthful elements of the land. The role model image of **the** *Military Governor, Col. Ojukwu,* with his intimidating profile as an Oxford University, London, graduate, and son of Africa's foremost millionaire of the time, reversed the negative impressions people had of the military as a profession of drop outs and zombies. Ojukwu's role model image, mythical competence, credible and selfless leadership, absolutely trusted by the people, the reality of the extermination agenda manifesting in the running cycle of atrocious attacks against the Easterners, necessitated the massive flocking of young men jostling to enlist into the Biafra military.

Ad hoc recruitment centers were populated, in large numbers, by young professionals, artisans, undergraduates, secondary school boys and girls, jostling to be enlisted. That there were no military jets, arms and ammunition did not bother them. All they wanted was to get enlisted into the army or the boys' company first, after all machetes and other traditional weapons of war were not scarce in the markets across the region.

The 66 Brigade of the Biafran Army at Nnobi was like other military Bases, a beehive of the recruitment activities. Young Chika and his younger brother, Benson, joined others to go for the enlistment into the Biafran Army. But lo! Chika was rejected on account of height and size, while his younger brother, Ben was enlisted. Chika refused to accept the rejection even when the recruiting officer had warned him not to come near the center again. On one occasion, he was frustrated by Chika's insistence that he chased him away with "Koboko" (horse whip). Chika felt a pang of humiliation and frustration, especially as his younger sibling was recruited and he, the elder, would be rejected. In his desperation to be enlisted into the Biafran military service like his peers, he dragged his father to go and plead with the Brigade Commander to enlist him. But the man was unyielding.

Why was Chika so desperate? He revealed that beyond the primary purpose of enlisting in the defense of threatened fatherland, joining the Army had its social attraction and prestige; this was the lure of the glamorous uniform, the honour and respect it commanded. In his comic Chief Zebrudaya language, Chika affirmed; attraction and prestige for the naïve young minds like him, this was the lure of the glamorous uniform, the honour and respect it commanded. In his comic Chief Zebrudaya language Chika tritely affirmed;

> *"Anybody that are join the army and are wear camouflage on the street are respected very well. We are does not know that bullet are kill people in the army. So dia for, all I am want then was to wear army uniform and enjoy my own respect like others! That's all"*

In truth, the lure of the army uniform was inspired by Col. Ojukwu who was a role model that attracted many of the young graduates of the time to join the army;

Ojukwu surely endeared himself to the people with his eloquence and oratory prowess. He manifested courage as a leader; and soldiers made him an idol of the East. His smart looks and carriage in the uniform brought glamour and glitz that stood him out.

However, for positive-minded Chika, being rejected in his bid to join the army to wear the camouflage did not mean the end of the road with destiny in the Army. Providence has more than one way of fulfilling one's innate desire. Chika recalled that after his failed bid to join the Army, he decided to enroll in a French language class primarily, to kill boredom. As fate would have it, he met many of his peers in the French class who mooted the idea of joining the Red Cross organization that was then training people on how to help people wounded at the war fronts or from air-raids in the villages.Through these ancillary services, Chika and his peers in the village were usefully engaged.

As the Eastern Region mobilized for an impending war, Chika's friend, one **Ogonna Agu** chanced upon a great idea of forming a Drama Club to entertain the soldiers at their base as they returned from the war fronts. Ogonna shared a lot in common with Chika as a drama enthusiast and very good in writing drama scripts. Like Chika, he was also in class four in his own school, Denis Memorial Grammar School (DMGS), Onitsha.

So, when Ogonna mooted the idea, Chika and his like that were in Drama Societies of their different schools wholly welcomed the idea. There and then, they formed **Two Cities Play House.** The Play House was so named to reflect the fact that some of them were from Nnobi, while the rest were from Awka Etiti. Having been denied the opportunity of joining the Biafran Army, the youngsters saw this as another smart way of getting close and identifying with the army, even though the ultimate essence of the drama was to provide psychological therapy to the fighting Biafran soldiers in their different formations.

The nine of them who formed the playhouse were;

Ogonna Agu, a student of Dennis Memorial Grammar School (DMGS), Onitsha who doubled as the leader of the group and the initiator of the idea.

Samuel Okpala, a staff of Barclays Bank (now Union Bank), Enugu

Fabian Okafor, a civil servant with the Eastern Region government

Emeka Okpala Eke, a student of Dennis Memorial Grammar School (DMGS), Onitsha.

Tony fez Ifezue, a civil Engineer.

Chika Chukwunonso Okpala, a student of Prince Memorial Secondary School, Onitsha.

Ifeoma Obosi, a student of Queens School, Lagos. **Chinwe Chikeluba,** a student of Queens School, Lagos.

Ifeoma Ezenyem, a student of Our Lady Secondary School, Nnobi.

As they rehearsed to launch the Two Cities Play House, a returnee from Lagos, who had the privilege of watching their rehearsals, suggested that they include a comedy teaser to lift their drama, since most of their audience may be illiterate soldiers. At this point, Chika's knowledge in comedy teaser gained from previewing films at Iweka Road, Onitsha, came in handy. They promptly adopted the idea and added a comedy teaser entitled, **"Mr. Okosisi",** as told by the Lagos returnee. According to the storyteller, Mr. Okosisi, an elderly man, had grandchildren who were visiting Nigeria from overseas to spend holiday with him. The comic part of the story was that these grandchildren mispronounced the old man's name, using foreign accent as "Oko-sai-sai"! And the old man did not find it funny as he shouted the correct name "Okosisi" at them! It was obvious that Chika would play the role of "Mr. Okosisi" in the teaser. Without a doubt, his excellence in comic act ended up making the teaser the driving force of their drama show. They first presented their drama to one Professor Umeh, a lecturer then with University of Nigeria, Enugu Campus. So thrilled at what he saw, Professor Umeh invited his kinsmen and indeed, anyone he could reach to come and see what these little boys were showcasing. At the end of their excellent performance, the highly pleased Professor Umeh, profusely commended them and showered fatherly blessings on the drama troupe.

After that test performance at Prof. Umeh's compound, Chika and his troupe moved to launch the show at 66 Brigade, Headquarters, Nnobi, the same Army base that refused them enlistment into the Army. In his Chief Zebrudaya comic language, Chika triumphantly stated;

> *On invitation, we was proceed to 66 Brigade Hqrs., Nnobi to perform our first play "The Frailties of man" by Ogo Agu and our famous Teaser "Oko-sai-sai (Okosisi). The same Brigade commander who was refusal to admit me in the army was full of praises and joy and was invitation us to come again and make the*

> *soldiers happy in two weeks' time. He was look at me and say" are you see what I am saw? That the play I am does are contributor to win the war effort. He was say if I was in the army would I have does thisgood play? You are plus include in the fight without gun. You are a soldier!*

The resounding success of their launch at the Army Base brought unprecedented open doors for them. Before long, they became quite popular and in hot demand for performances. The drama show took the troupe to different army formations in almost all the Army Brigades under the 11 Divisions, as well as many cities such as Nnewi that were not under siege or captured by the Federal troops. They were equally invited to perform and entertain the Biafran Military High Command at the Divisional Headquarters, Akabo, Owerri, where Gen. Phillip Effiong lavished them with gifts and commendations.

And so, it came to pass that without army uniform, Chika and his troupe found themselves playing their own very critical roles in the Army, just as those in uniform were playing theirs in the general war efforts of Biafra. As a matter of fact, with their excellent drama, Chika and his troupe had, inadvertently, joined the Army, with their drama and distinguished themselves as glorious combatants, though in the frontiers of entertainment and re-psyching the wounded and traumatized survivors of the war. This marked the beginning of Chika's destiny with comedy and lifetime march to fame and greatness with drama and acting.

2.3 COMING TO ENUGU AFTER THE WAR

As the weeks rolled by into months, and months into years, the war raged on; the three divisions of the Federal forces remained progressive in overrunning and conquering the Biafran territories. The infant Republic began to shrink under the impact of the pounding shelling power of heavy artilleries, complemented adequately with ceaseless booms of heavy machine guns.

For Chika and the troupe, the deteriorating situation equally affected the run of things for them. Movement to places to stage drama shows were increasingly becoming too dangerous a venture to make, with the indiscriminate attacks and regular air raids on public places. This made public gatherings of any kind dangerous. Under the prevailing circumstances, bookings for performances were becoming very rare. Gradually and quietly, they unceremoniously disbanded.

It was just a matter of time for the dreaded, but necessary tragic end to eventualy come on January 15, 1970 as the Eastern Region, then named the Republic of Biafra, surrendered to Federal Forces. For Chika and his friends, the tragic end of the war equally marked the informal fall of the curtain, on the promising Two Cities Play House. It was an unspoken situation of;

> *To your homes O 'comrades and to your parents, (for those whose parents survived the perilous times) Such was the situation we found ourselves when the war ended and almost everybody was rushing to Enugu to look for what to do to feed famil y*

Chika recalled. He was about eighteen and a half years old then and joined in the mad rush. When he got into Enugu, it dawned on him that he knew nobody in Enugu, and had no where to sleep. How was he going to survive and get on with life in the city? Just as he was wondering over his helpless situation, he remembered his previous engagement with Red Cross back in Nnobi. Luckily, he found his Red Cross identity card in his pocket and walked straight to the Red Cross Headquarters at Okpara Avenue. After Introducing himself and presenting his ID card, the officer in-charge heartily welcomed him and promptly assigned him to be in-charge of clinic kitchen; and distribute free cooked food rations to returnees from the war.

A man's destiny never fails him, when his God is with him. Chika Okpala's God was with him always. At this point, he was a manifestation of Prince Nicco Mbaga's proverbial lyrics; **"cow wey no get tail na God de drive am flies."** But God was not done yet with Chika! Miraclously, Ogonna Agu resurfaced in Enugu too. Yes, same Ogonna Agu, who brought the idea of the drama, Two Cities Play House that gave them fame and blessings; showed up at that critical moment again. Ogonna, who by all indications was his destiny helper providentially surfaced, this time, to solve the accommodation puzzle at Enugu for Chika. Testifying to this Chika said;

> *I did that (serving people food) for two hours and I was asked to take a seat and have my meal. As I sat to eat, look at Ogonna Agu, my playmate at Two Cities Play house who also came to eat. When the kitchen closed by 7 PM, we collected our dinner and I followed him to No.33 Zik Avenue where he lived. Not too long after, the owner of the accommodation came in and he was a member of our Two Cities Play house at Nnobi. Tony Ifezue is his name. He was married to Ogonna 's younger sister. I felt at home with them. At the end of every two weeks, I was paid with half bag of rice, half bag of beans, half bag of stockfish (Okproko), and half bag of salt.*

From then on, the hassle of living as a responsible adult away from the protective tutelage of his parents began for Chika. Many opportunities were there in Enugu under Ukpabi Asika as the Administrator of East Central State, but then, there was this ostensive air of uncertainty and edgy feelings of the post-war experience. So, the normal everyday life was lived with tacit caution. Nevertheless, as more returnees flocked in daily, the gregarious bustles of life in the city began to pick up.

Chika got another opportunity to work at the Enugu campus of UNN. It was at this point that he met Prof. Tim Uzodimma Nwala and Prof. Emeka Okpara. Both were in-charge of a project for undergraduates to clean up the mess made in the campus by the Federal troops who camped there after the fall of Enugu in October 1967. He sought to join and they registered him. The project was called "Food for work" programme." I was paid the same thing as I got from the Red Cross clinic kitchen. So there was enough food for me and enough to send to my parents and siblings at home."

"Quest cera cera;" the French would say. And truly, "whatever would be, would be," in the life of a man of destiny. In His mysterious ways, the Lord has a way of making what would be to be in our lives. Being an actor apparently had become a manifest destiny for Chika; just like the wartime mantra of the Federal troops; "to keep Nigeria one is a task that must be done". It seemed Chika's Chi had so avowed; "to be an actor is a task that must be accomplished in his life." And once again, Ogonna, the recurrent destiny messenger in his life, came home with the message that there was drama rehearsals going on at the British Council, Ogui Road, Enugu. The rehearsals were by very senior civil servants, and he wanted Chika to join the rehearsals. Without much ado, Chika promptly followed Ogonna to see what the whole thing was about. The group in question, named **Hill Top Arts Theatre,** was rehearsing **"Sons and Daughters,"** a very fascinating story by **J.C. Degraft**, a Ghanaian playwright.

After the rehearsals, Ogonna introduced himself to the producer, Mr. James Iroha (OON), the indefatigable playwright and actor- producer, It was equally at that rehearsal that he met Mrs. Elizabeth Okaro and Chris Ofordile, who later became the Director General of the East Central State Broadcasting Service (ECBS). Even when all the roles had been assigned out, Mr. Iroha still had to do something for him. Chika was assigned to play a stand-by role of Awureh, already assigned to Bede Nnamdi Olebara. Chika made such a huge success of his trial role as a stand-by cast in a manner that highly impressed Mr. Iroha. He promptly offered him another role to play for him in a radio play he wrote and produced at the ECBS. The programme was a quarter hour chit-chat and jokes format, entitled **"In a Lighter Mood."** Iroha's offer to Chika as a regular feature, in a radio drama, marked the beginning of his journey into the broadcasting world in 1971. Chika recalled;

> *The East Central State Government under the Sole Administrator, Mr. Ukpabi Asika invited us to a command performance at the Government House, Enugu. After the performance, the Sole Administrator extolled our performance and the ingenuity of the producer/Director, James Iroha OON. He promised to take us to places.*
>
> *It wasn't two weeks, an invitation to perform at the Nigeria Army Week at Kaduna came from the Sole Administrator, for our troupe to travel with him in a white train to Kaduna.*
> *For me, it was a big surprise and fulfilling engagement. I had never traveled beyond the shores of Ahoada, Porthcourt and Onitsha.*
> *When the news came that we would travel by "white Train" to*

Kaduna, my excitement was beyond imagination. I had never taken train before not to talk of white train with the Sole Administrator. On the appointed date, we boarded the white train straight to Kaduna. At Kaduna, we were checked into Hamdala Hotels, a Five Star Hotel. I was checked into a suit, so also every member of the troupe.

That was my first time of meeting one on one those Army Generals that fought against Biafra people like Gen. TY Danjuma, Gen Garuba, Gen Domkat Bali,etc. they were very friendly. They gave us a lot of gifts including clothing, shoes, flasks etc. We spent 2 weeks at Hamdala Hotels Kaduna and performed four times. All of us artistes and crew were at our best. We all came back at the end of the trip safely and fulfilled. Two weeks later another invitation came from the Head of State, General Yakubu Gowon to come for a command performance at Dodan Barracks Lagos, the seat of Nigerian Government.
This time a presidential jet was sent to us here in Enugu. At Dodan Barracks Lagos, the seat of power, I was privileged to shake hands with General Gowon, the Head of State and members of the Supreme Military Council.

It is worthy of note that these rehearsals/drama performances did not stop Chika's regular work with Red Cross and Enugu campus. While doing the Enugu campus cleaner job, he noticed that some lecturers were holding extra moral lessons in the campus. He took interest and registered for the lessons. Incidentally, his bosom friend, Ogonna had been returned back to school at the DMGS, Onitsha, by his parents. Unlike Ogonna, Chika's parents were unable to return him back to school; but he therefore took a consolatory solace in the extra moral lessons to improve his education and measure up with his peers. The campus lessons were additional self-embraced burden. This changed his daily routine to; working with the Red Cross clinic kitchen in the morning, the cleaning job at Enugu Campus in the afternoon, and then at nightfall, he went for the extra moral lessons at the same Enugu campus. As time rolled by, he got engaged by some companies such as M. A. Nwabude and Sons Building & Construction Company, as Accounts Supervisor and Secretary between 1971/72. From there he moved on to join Press Oil Nigeria Ltd, Enugu also as Accounts- Supervisor and Secretary later that same year in 1972. The following year, in 1973, Chika joined GION Nigeria Ltd, one of the biggest furniture manufacturing companies, in Enugu. He was the company's Accounts Supervisor and Public Relations Officer (PRO).

He remained with this company up to 1976 when new states were created, which necessitated the relocation of the *Masquerade TVShow,* in which he played a part at Aba, in the newly created Imo State. When it became very expedient to have him relocate to Aba for this show, the Chief Executive Officer of his company. who had already become very proud and supportive of him was quite cooperative and graciously released him on demand to NTA, Aba; before he was eventually employed formally into the Federal Service through NTA Channel 6, Aba.

2.4 BREAKING INTO BROADCASTING

There is an Igbo saying; *When one says yes! His god will equally say yes to his fate.* For Chika Chukwunonso Okpala, his lure to films right from his toddler years in the primary school at Ahoada, through secondary school at Onitsha, and his tenacious inclination and stellar performance in acting everywhere he went, showed more than anything that in body, soul and spirit Chika had destiny with drama and acting. Simply put, he is a born actor, a thespian of a rare stock made by nature. No little wonder he towers over and above his peers as the main act in the industry.

Recall that his father, in words and deliberate action, dissuaded him from the fantasy world of films and acting; as he desperately wanted to have a banker son in Chika. Part of his futile effort to change young Chika's career was sending him out of Ahoada to live with an ex-serviceman as a house boy at Joinkarama, just to banish him from his friends and film shows which he believed was a distraction. Even when Chika passed his entrance exam to many secondary schools, his father chose a commercial secondary school against the conventional grammar school out of the lot. This was to ensure that Chika studied the relevant subjects that were requisite for his study of banking in the university.

Chika did not resist his father, but his *chi* (guardian god) ensured that his star and destiny were not dimmed. The civil war that truncated Chika's secondary education and financially deterred his father from returning him to finish school, after the war, was in the major change in the trajectory of his life.

Destined for drama and acting, Chika progressed with every opportunity – from the amateur **Two Cities Play House** in Nnobi to chancing upon the professionals' **Hilltop Arts Theatre** in

Enugu, and finally, the mentorship of Mr. James Iroha, the horizon expanded for Chika

It is worthy of note that Chika intuitively realized that these invitations for command performances in Kaduna and Lagos were part of the reconciliatory efforts by the Federal Military Government under General Yakubu Gowon, to reintegrate the Igbos back to the federation. This noble intention by General Gowon was not lost on the astute producer, James Iroha (OON), who creatively saw dramatic expressions in Gowon's *"No victor No vanquished"* declaration coupled with the well- intentioned *"three-R policy"* of *Reconciliation, Reintegration* and *Rehabilitation* of the Nigerians

Expectedly, the onus of interpreting and bringing this noble policy down to the understanding of the people was that of the broadcast media – radio and later TV through drama. In response James Iroha latched onto this responsibility with deep cognizance of the mood the war wrecked on eastern audience.

Like Goerge Orwell did in defunct Communist Soviets with his **Animal Farm,** Iroha chose to go satirical. And as a great playwright, he couched the messages of his drama productions to promote the government's postwar policies, thus highlighting, through the medium of satire/comedy, the frustrations and expectations of war returnees.

2.5 THE MAKING OF THE NEW MASQUERADE & ZEBRUDAYA

While the post-war reconstruction of the burnt down East Central Broadcasting Service (ECBS) facilities commenced, Mr. James Iroha, the talented producer/playwright of ECBS also embarked on a psychological reconstruction of the psyche of the defeated Easterners, bringing hope, reassurances, and revival through the medium of drama and comedy to the sober and sullen people. The idea was to mask the desperate situation with laughter and satire as the people lifted themselves up to regain their productive power. Mr. Iroha may not have envisaged the global success the Masquerade was to become, but he inadvertently, in actions and deeds, created and conceptualized the Masquerade and Chief Zebrudaya that dominated the broadcast world for decades.

The journey began with a quarter of an hour chit-chat/jokes radio programme, created and produced by Mr. Iroha, titled, **In A Lighter Mood,** in which the lead character was *Chief Jesophat Okoro Nwogbo, alias 4.30.* Chika recalled that in this all- important radio drama, Iroha initially auditioned and cast him to play the part of **Natty,** who by instinct visits Chief Nwogbo's home whenever food is ready at the table. The drama blended well with the radio chit-chat and jokes programme.

Chika recalled amusingly;

I played the role well, considering my stature then, very slim and hungry looking.

The drama series was on air uninterrupted for months until there was a misunderstanding between the producer, Mr. Iroha and **Nsofor Obua,** who acted Chief Jesophat Okoro Nwogbo and **Davis Offor**, who played the part of Clarus Mgbojikwe of Ndi Olumbe. The two artistes absconded from rehearsals and recordings for three weeks. This embarrassingly frustrated and held up the productions and airing of the weekly programme.

In his quest for replacement of the two characters, a distraught

Iroha was advised to try Chika in the role of **Chief Jesophat Okoro Nwogbo, alias 4:30,** given Chika's voice carriage. This trial swap of roles was quite successful, drawing positive audience ratings, acceptance and commendation. Chika was therefore made to retain the role permanently cast, while another artiste, **Romanus Amuta** was auditioned to replace him as Natty.

That misunderstanding also informed the introduction of a new character in the drama - **Giringory Akabogu** of Ikot 4.

Even when Mr. Iroha later reconciled with these artistes, Chika was not relieved of the role as he continued to play Chief Nwogbo. This marked the birth of the famous TV Masquerade that later mutated to the all-time great satirical comic drama series to run on Nigeria's national television network – NTA; as well as Chika's induction into professional acting and broadcasting.

As providence would have it, the reconciliation of Nsofor Obua and Davis Ofor with Mr. Iroha (OON) coincided with the advent of television services for the East Central State Broadcasting Service (ECBS) leading to a combined radio and TV services that offered abundant opportunities for staff, artistes and audience. Instantly, another weekly drama, **Wind vs Polygamy** was born**,** written by **Obi Egbuna** for the TV audience of the station. James Iroha was also the producer. Mr. Egbunna, who was Director of Writers' Workshop East Central State, was drafted in as the Director of the ECBS-TV. The prolific writer came with the policy that no actor should take up two major roles in the two leading Radio and TV drama programmes - *Wind vs Polygamy* and *"In a Lighter Mood"* which was then renamed, "**Masquerade.**" The name, Masquerade, has cultural and satirical underlining among Igbo people, who considered masquerades as ancestral spirits come alive in the communities. Beyond entertainment, masquerades have other esoteric duties and jurisprudential powers to speak truth to powers and equally condemn the ills of society without fear of any consequences. With these changes, the name of the lead character, Chief Jesophat Okoro Nwogbo was changed to Chief Zebrudaya Okoroigwe Nwogbo, alias 4.30. Nsofor Obua was assigned the lead role of Chief Ozuomba in the *Winds vs Polygamy*, while Chika Okpala played Chief Zebrudaya Okoroigwe Nwogbo alias 4.30 in the *Masquerade*. Chika declared;

> *Well, there were others who played the role of Chief Zebrudaya before me. As I mentioned earlier, the role began as Chief Josephat Okoro Nwogbo.*
>
> *Mr. Nwora Asika was the first cast, followed by Chief Pete Edochie. They were both highly trained English Announcers and were using their Queen's English diction in acting the role and it wasn't actually jelling with the down to earth comic perspective of the drama. So they were not ranking well in the weekly postmortem of the drama.*

Corroborating Chika's assertion, Chief Pete Edochie, who earlier played the same role stated; "As a matter of fact, when we created Masquerade, the very first Chief Zebrudaya was Nwora Asika. Nwora did a couple of episodes. On the day he (Nwora) did not come, there was a very young man who volunteered to try, and that young man was Chika Okpala. Chika was so young that we required making him up. And for him to look the part, we gave him the tommy. Chika proved a very creative young man. He converted his limitations into an asset. That's why I must always congratulate him"

Chika showed determination to step into the larger shoes of those polished English-speaking grand masters of the game and with a rare acting mettle to dethrone them to take over the major role. Attesting again, Chief Edochie affirmed; "I must candidly add that, by the time Chika took over that production, his English was not very good, and like I said, he converted that to an asset . . . I remember the first time he wanted to pronounce "Chief" he said "Chieef." We felt as though he was being whimsical. After some time, it became clear that there was no need for Nwora Asika to go back to that programme. Chika had given that role an identity that nobody could challenge and he became an instant celebrity, a very big superstar"

To clinch the role and prove the huge success he has made of the Masquerade and himself, Chika revealed;

> *I never missed the rehearsals of both In a Lighter Mood changed to The Masquerade as well as the writers' workshop program under Mr. Obi B. Egbuna. Winds v. polygamy, was the writer's workshop maiden drama production. In the Winds vs. Polygamy, I was cast to play the role of a poor hunter, challenging an honourable member of parliament making passes at my daughter, Elena.*
>
> *When the ECBS-TV which was burnt down during the war was reactivated in 1974, both Masquerade and Winds vs Polygamy, the two powerful plays were lifted unto television. We moved Wind versus Polygamy on stage, performed in Enugu and Port Harcourt. For the Masquerade, we performed on stage in many cities in Nigeria and abroad. It wasn't too long Masquerade became overwhelmingly popular in Nigeria and in the Diaspora.*

Indeed, the popularity of the Masquerade was such that the audio episodes were also produced in record albums and cassette tapes that sold massively nationwide and beyond. Therefore, right from its conception and birth, **The Masquerade**, produced by an outstanding producer and performer of the hue of an Officer of the Order of the Niger (OON), James Iroha, with a crop of superlative artistes of inimitable qualities, were destined for greatness

2.6 SELLING FEATURES OF THE MASQUERADE

The Masquerade was a delight to behold on stage; just as it proved more wondrous and glamorous on TV, with a universal audience appeal. Everything about the Masquerade was unique – the characterization, choice of cast, the names given to these characters each with a comic suffix or alias, and a dash of profound creativity born of a professional creator glorious in his act. As Chika confirmed;

> *It was the person who wrote the play, James Iroha, who was also the producer that gave the names of the characters and their aliases. Nobody was allowed to add alias to his or her name by himself or herself. You could only add either Prince or Chief to your name.*

Behold these glorious Casts with their magnificent names and flowery aliases; CHIKA OKPALA - **Chief Zebrudaya Okoroigwe Nwogbo – alias 4.30, Chief his Royal palmwine powerless;** He had four wives, but lived with one at a time, ensuring none met the other in his house. These wives were: **Mrs. Celina Ogbodia Nwaogbo**, the first wife (she later left for the USA). The second wife was **Madam Gctrude Appolonia Godgive Nwogbo of Umudele, in Ukwa Divide**. She was a bar owner (beer parlour) where Chief Zebrudayia spent his evenings drinking palm wine which he described as; *"going to consummate his tombo-liquor from 4:30 pm to 4:30 am"*. She was called Madam True Word of the Bar in Enugu. The third wife, who had the shortest span, was **Mrs. Magadalyn Nwogbo;** and she was replaced by the most memorable of these wives; **Mrsisim Ovularia Urediya Nwogbo - alias G4 of Bakana via Isiokpo in Ikwere Pracourt; the**

granddaughter of Izombe, the great panel beater, played by the adorable, **LIZZY EVOEME**,

Mrsisim Ovularia was the 4th and longest serving wife of Chief Zebrudaya;

> *She are warn me warning that any day I am talk too much talkative of abuse to her, she will proceed with alacrity to call her father who are panel beater to panel beat my mouth. So I am took careful to talk to her to put my mouth in the permanent condition of suum*

The hilarious Zebrudaya would add, feigning fear and helplessness before her.

Chief's house boys were **Davis Offor** - **Clarus Mgbojikwe of Ndiolumbe,** the senior houseboy, cunning and mischievous, always taking advantage of the naïve junior house boy; **Gringory Akabogu of Ikot 4,** *the honourable poor man of Europia* – played by the producer himself**, James Iroha.** For national diversity, Chief Zebrudaya had a Yoruba friend and member of the community by the name**, Olabisi Ajiboye** of **Ijebu Remo,** played by **Maxwell Elenmuo.** He is today a university teacher, and one of the surviving pioneer members of the Masquerade as at this writing. Upon his departure for the USA, **Claudus Eke** replaced him and changed the name, Olabisi Ajiboye to the cantankerous and petulant Prince Dr. Jegede Shokoya; the grandson of Idi of Idi Araba.

Jegede's first wife in the drama was **Akpenor, alias hot water,** played by **Christy Essien Igbokwe.** When Christy eased off the drama rehearsals to concentrate on her fledgling music career, she was replaced by **Sikira.** Sirika's period in the drama was also shortlived as she was replaced by **Ramota,** *alias ice water,* played by **VERO NJOKU. Romanus Amuta,** played

Natty, Okosisi, the inglorious hungry-looking gluttonous character that by dint of regular coincidences always arrived when meals were served in Chief Zebrudaya's house and never said no to invitations to join the table.

There were some other sub-casts such as; **Mazi Okoro Maduekwe;** played by **Emmanuel Nwaogwu. Polycarp Anusionwu** and **Peter Uwadineke,** who at various times, played the role of **Mallam Shehu Adamu, the Hausa member of the Masquerade community,** accentuating the need for national unity.

Later in the drama, when the name was changed to New Masquerade on NTA Network, there was Tony Akposheri, who played **Zaki**; the young guy man in the community. Expectedly, there were some unseen characters that were mentioned in the drama. For instance, no one ever saw Chief Zebrudaya's children, but they existed in the drama script and often mentioned. They were there; **Benji Nwam Nwogbo** and **Gilbert Nwam Nwogbo** were his sons. **Agnes**, who was fondly refered to as **Agie Nwam Nwogbo, Philo Nwam Nwogbo** and **Mgbafor Afolene Nwogbo** were his daughters. **Singlton** was his grandson from Benji. Jegede also had a son, **Atonda**. Natty's wife was **Ngarasi**. The manner of pronouncing these names and their aliases with their excellent voice carriages gave them great importance in the ears and minds of the audience. This essentially accentuated the entertainment and onomatopoeic values and effects. The sound of the name of the lead actor **Chief Zebrudaya,** conjures some mythical aura around the character which tend to remind one of the super human powers and invincibility stature therein. The name, ZEBRUDAYA, remains urbanely unique to the comic drama, the Masquerade as conceived by James Iroha, Chika's mentor of all times.

In reflection, Chika affirmed;

As said earlier, the name - Zebrudaya was given by James Iroha himself and he never told us how he came by that name. I asked him severally and he refused to tell me where he got the name from. And that's how the name continued and has remained stuck with me for life and eternally to the drama.

2.7 THE UNIQUE LANGUAGE

Beyond the unique qualities and sensation of the names of the casts, one other enduring and endearing entertainment values of the Masquerade is the language of communication by the lead character, Chief Zebrudaya. It was not unexpected to observe, across Africa, the cultural impact of colonialism in the emergence of a different type of language as the indigenous people grappled with the "whiteman's mother tongue" The resultant effect was a convenient marriage between vernacular and English language (Anglophone colonies) aided by non-verbal signs to ensure the recipient of communication understood the message. In Nigeria, especially in the southern part, it is called Pidgin English, in Sierra Leone, it is Creole and a different variant of pidgin in Anglophone part of Cameroon.

But Chief Zebrudaya's language is not entirely pidgn English but a combination of everything – adulterated good English with the use of present, past, and continuous tenses all in one sentence, pidgin, infusion *The Man and Legend of New Masquerade:* **Zebrudaya** of many vernacular languages and sparse French (especially Ovuleria). For national cohesion, which was one of the objectives of the drama, all the major ethnic nationalities in Nigeria were represented as characters, and they acted their roles and spoke their lines in the dialectal intonation of their ethnicity. For instance, Clarus Mgboji kwe, an Igboman, serving as senior houseboy, exhibited that domineering, leader-in-the-pack tendencies of Igbo. On the other hand, simple-minded and humorous Giringory Akabogu, in manners and voice, reflected a typical houseboy of an Efik-Ibibio origin. Just like Prince Dr. Jegede Shokoya and his wife, Akpenor (later replaced by Ramota), did not disappoint in projecting the haughty Yoruba people.

It is to the eternal credit of the producer of the Masquerade, James Iroha, who created the multi-linguist approach for every role and every character in the drama. This includes that of the main actor, Chief Zebrudaya Okoroigwe Nwogbo, alias 4.30; whose manner of speaking became sensational with the viewers and enjoyed a followership, in what could be termed "Zebrudayic" iconic and humorous grammar. It needs emphasizing that Chika Okpala's unique language that has become his trademark and a major selling feature of his role in the drama was predestined. This is given the story he told of his beloved father who came about such manner of communication in his daily transactions with non-English speaking foreign customers in his textile shop at the main Market Onitsha.

Recall that Chika's fascination with the language was two-pronged; first, the fact that his illiterate father could close deals with well-spoken foreign traders and make money enough to build houses in the village. Secondly, he concluded that since the language was good for business, it may well be good for school assignment; and so wrote an essay with the jargons that got him severely punished. It can best be described as divine that Chika found an acting role that permitted him to speak the hitherto rejected language and earn global acclaim. No wonder he became such a natural actor with the role and language as Davis Offor aka CLARIUS MGBOJIKWE confirmed;

> *The language became part of him and then he fitted in into the character himself very well. We had Obi Egbuna, who was Director, Writers' Workshop, where . . . we were acting before. This man Obi Egbuna, was so happy with the program, he said what he loved most was how the English language was being bastardized, that thing made him love the program. You know, so that is it.*

Davis Ofor is today an ordained priest of the Atherius Churches Ministries Worldwide.

It is also a common fact of life that every phenomenon has its beautiful and ugly sides, while this unique language factor remained one of the unique selling points of the powerful sitcom, it had dissenting echoes of repudiation from some quarters. In her own attestation on this language factor of the Masquerade, one of the surviving main casts of the comedy, Chief Lizzy Evoeme aka Mrsisim Ovularia Urediya Nwogbo enthusiastically stated; Ahhmm! There's a proverb in Ngwa dialect they say; **"oha abughiuto", "Oha abughi iro",** Not everybody will like you. And not everybody will hate you, or what you are doing. People were hailing the New Masquerade. "Ooh! That programme!" But not everybody liked us. Some didn't like the language. For instance, when Jegede was there, and was speaking his Yoruba, a lot of Yoruba people didn't like him. They said he was bastardizing the language. When Zebrudaya speaks his English, a lot of English Nigerians or Nigerian English men said he was killing the English language. Some people saw Ovularia as a peacock. So, it was individualistic according to Oyibo grammarians.

You know, so, I cannot generalize. It was a case of you like some, you don't like some!

It is equally pertinent to place on record here that generating scripts and ideas for high-class productions like the Masquerade was never a monopoly of any single writer. The major scriptwriters were: James Iroha (OON), the grand creator and producer of the programe, Davis Offor, Chika Okpala, Peter Eneh, Ukwu Rocks, Emma Chris, Obi-Rapu, Chris Oluka, Nkem Owoh (the famous Marcus Nwaezeigwe/Osuoffia Ezeigbo), Fabian Adibe etc.

On his part, Ukwu Rocks. son of Igbere land, veered off into politics and rose to become the Chairman, Bende Local Government Area of Abia State, and later Commissioner for Information in Abia State.

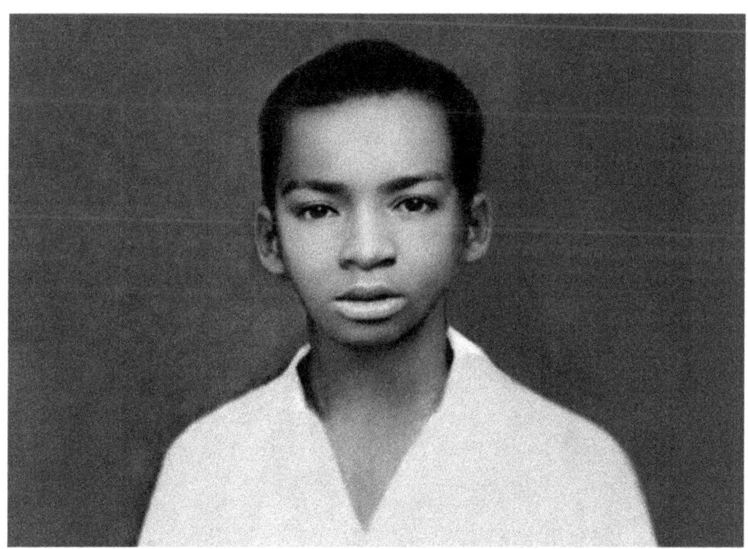

1960's Chika Chukwunonso Okpala

1995 Chief Daniel Okpala (Ezeogomegbunam) & Lolo Ezinne Urunwa Okpala

Chief Chika & Lolo Christy Okpala after an event

1995 Lolo Ezinne Gladys Okpala and Amb. Chief Chika Okpala

1981 Chika and Christy Okpala wedded at Our Lady of Lourdes Catholic Church, Aba

1981 Young Chief Chika and his wife Christy Ebele Omunuzuo Okpala

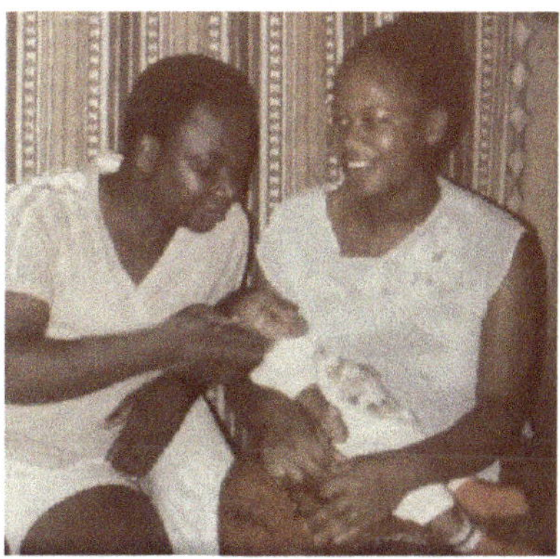

1983 Chief Chika & his wife Christy with their new baby Afam Okpala

2020 Chief Chika and Lolo Christy Okpala with their children, Afam Henry Okpala and Ogechukwu Anita Okpala in a family photograph

Silver Jubilee of Television in Nigeria Producer Award

The author's perception of the New Masquerade in 1984

Symbols of the New Masquerade with Edikwansa jingle

2013; Chief Chika Okpala and Camilla Mberekpa in a scene of a play titled man of integrity by Chika Okpala

1999 Chief Zebrudaya Alias 4 30 with Major cast of New Masquerade on set

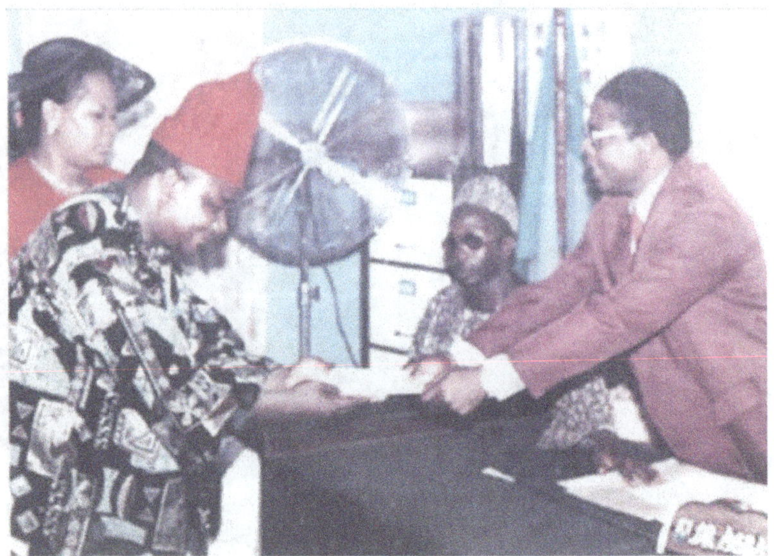

1999 Chief Chika with wife Christy Okpala receiving MFR award by Federal Govt of Nigeria from Dr. Agbasi, Idemili South LG Chairman

Chief Chika Okpala displaying his Nigeria Film Corporation Award, he dedicated to Anambra State Goernment

Chief Chika Okpala in warm handshake with former President Yahya Jammeh of the Gambia during an official visit to Gambia

"Look" he began asking us to sit. "I've got a friend, Joseph Momoh who will be sworn in as president of Sierra Leone in five days. "So, go and get ready with your team and best episodes," he said to me. "You 're going to Sierra Leone to perform for my friend"

"Yes, Sir" I said, and we left.

A series of excellent performances in the longest running television comedy in Nigeria

1985; Chief Zebrudaya and Ovularia on set

1985 Chief ZB, Ovularia and Jegede on set to bail Natty

ZB and Jegede bails Natty from prison

1984; Chief ZB Alias 4:30 with New Masquerade principal characters

1984; Zebrudaya and New Masquerade cast playing on conjunctivitis

Ambasador Chief Chika Okpala chairing a comedy conference

Zebrudaya, Ovularia and Seracus after pose production

2017; Chief Chika Okpala, MON, MFR, FTA graduation at Noun University, Abuja Campus

1989 Chika Okpala conducting writers workshop for New Masquerade

1988 Chief Zebrudaya positioning camera to shoot an advert

Chief Zebrudaya inspects camera perspective before shoot

Zebrudaya with briefcase and his Benze

2023; Signing this book agreement at Zodiac Studios

Zebrudaya in celebrated episodes

Zebrudaya a master of humor

ZB, Star Character in Failed Investment | Mama Gee & Zebrudaya Movie

Zebrudaya's Epic Visit to USA

Chief Zebrudaya at Kennedy Space Center TX & Times Square NY USA

Camera man shooting a scene from the film "Cultures" with Chief ZB as Principal character, written and produced by Oliver Mbamara Esq. Pic -r Chief Zebrudaya, pose for pic after an interview in Carteret NJ with Alex Iheke Igbo Basics,Oliver Mbamara, Isaac Iheke and Felix Nnorom

ZB at the house of his son, played by Oliver Mbamara in Carteret NJ

l -ZB rehearsing his script r- Zebrudaya interview by Igbo Basics, NJ USA

2023 Chief Chika Okpala discussing book project

2022 Ovularia interview in Port Harcourt

2022 Clarus interview for this book at Aba

January 5, 2021 Alexander Iheke (Opiegbe) visited Chief Chika Okpala (ZB) and Lolo Christy Okpala at Zodiac Studios for purpose of this book

ZB reviews draft copy of the book while Lolo Okpala admires the process graciously

PART THREE

The Nigeria Television Authority (NTA)

3.1 From Regional to National STAR

3.2 Advent of The NTA

3.3 The Golden Era of Radio and TV

3.4 Life After NTA & The Birth of Zodiak Brains

Chapter 3

FROM REGIONAL TO NATIONAL STAR

A popular Igbo adage says; "na bu enyi kaa, adu ya akaa." Meaning "when the elephant matures, its tusks matures as well" Given his soaring popularity on the screen, Chika Chukwunonso Okpala was by all means a rising star in the East. The year 1976 was significant and marked another turning point in his acting vocation. General Murtala Muhammed, who came to power the previous year on July 29, 1975, as Nigeria's third military head of state, created seven new states in the country on February 03, 1976, thus elevating Nigeria to a 19 state federation:

North Eastern State was split into; Gongola State, with Yola as capital; Borno State, with Maidugiri as capital; and Bauchi State, with Bauchi as capital.

North Western State was split into; Kano State, with Kano City as capital; and Kwara State, with Ilorin as Capital.

Western State was spilt into; Ondo State, with Akure as capital; Ogun State, with Abeokuta as capital; and Oyo State, with Ibadan as capital.

East Central State was spilt into; Anambra State, with Enugu as capital; and Imo State, with Owerri as capital.

Benue-Plateau State was split into Benue State, with Makurdi as capital; and Plateau State, with Jos as capital

Another remarkable fact of this state creation exercise by Gen. Muhammed was the renaming of states, across the Federation, to reflect cultural and ancestral linkages; "This was to erase memories of past political ties and emotional attachments", the General clarified. Consequently, South Eastern State changed to Cross River State, with Calabar as Capital.

North Central State changed to Kaduna State, with Kaduna as capital.

Midwestern State changed to Bendel State, with Benin City as capital.

Lagos, the then Federal Capital Territory, became a state, with Ikeja as capital.

Rivers State remained, with Port Harcourt as capital.

The state creation in 1976 resulted in unprecedented chain of events, both positive and negative depending on one's interpretation. The cataclysmic effect was evident in all facets of public and civil service operation culminating in asset sharing, human resource re-assessment, and eventual relocation of indigenes to their new state, for instance, movement from Enugu (Anambra State) to Owerri (Imo State). However, Imo indigenes working in ECBS, Enugu were given the option to relocate to Imo Broadcasting TV, Aba (which was reactivated even before ECBS TV, Enugu), or remain in ECBS, Enugu. Interestingly, virtually all the Imo indigenes in ECBS, Enugu opted to go to Imo, including, James Iroha, the grand master producer of the Masquerade.

Similarly, all the artistes in the Masquerade TV programme came from Imo, except for Chika, and Romanus Amuta (Naaty).

Meanwhile, because Chika was functioning as a guest artiste and was from the new Anambra, he was granted the privilege to choose anywhere he wished and/or where his services were needed.

Beyond the controversies thrown up by the creation of new state, one of the major concerns of the producer, cast and teeming fans of the Masquerade programme was the survival of the programme. Indeed, a lot of concession, realignment and ground shifting had to occur, among the cast and crew, in order to keep the programme on air.

Mr. Iroha shepherded and nurtured this programme to its all-time great as the number one TV drama show that kept Nigerians, east and south of the Niger glued to their TV sets weekly.

On each day of the programme, homes with TV sets, had to put up with inconveniences of large crowd of people from the neighbourhood, who would cluster their windows and every space that gave them sight of the TV to watch the programme. Every episode was worth the stress. Needless to mention that the casts became instant household names. In what could be described as a fulfillment of childhood dream, kids narrated, with glee, every episode of Masquerade and Chief Zebrudaya's comic antics, the same way Chika, hitherto, took the story of John Wayne films to his primary school friends back in Ahoada.

Two years after the creation of states came yet another significant turning point for Chika in 1978. His master and mentor, James Iroha, OON resigned from the services of NTA and left the production of the programmme to take up higher responsibilities in the newly created state broadcaster, Imo State Broadcasting Service in Owerri, the state capital.

Chika and Davis Offor, without any warning, suddenly found

themselves saddled with the responsibility of scripting and producing the weekly Masquerade TV programme. It was surely not an easy task to fit into the big shoes of the grand master by his pupils. Nevertheless, it's a fact that every headmaster was once a pupil, and so, all pupils would surely grow to be headmasters especially, those who have both the head and hue of their headmasters. Chika and Davis did not disappoint as they lived up to their new role; hence the programme sustained its verve and progress through the years.

However, at the dawn of the 1 980s, Chika was posted to Jos to join the NTA production crew of Cock Crow at Dawn, another glorious soap opera that stirred ripples in the land from the plateau. Chika played the role of Baba Asabe in the star-studded programme while working as production Manager under Mr. Peter Igho, the Executive Producer/Director of the Cock Crown at Dawn Programme.

Starring in the programme, which was a Network broadcast, gave Chika a taste of a national stardom; thus migrating from regional limelight into the realms of national stars.

He returned to NTA ABA three years later in 1983. This time he and Davis Offor had an opportunity to improve on their education. They got a grant to run remedial courses that would qualify them for a degree programme in Theatre Arts at Tedem University, Owerri. This grant came from magnanimous Dr. Nnana Ukaegbu, the Proprietor of Tedem - Imo Techolongy, University Imerienwe, Owerri.

One year into this programme came the December 31, 1984 coup that ushered in the duo of General Mohammadu Buhari and General Tunde Idiagbon to power. One of those sweeping changes that came with that government that affected Chika and others was the proscription of all private universities in Nigeria, including Tedem, thereby truncating their remedial programme. Coincidentally too, the NTA headquarters sent for Chika, directing him to report to the national programmes headquarters, Victoria Island, Lagos where Mr. Peter Igho had assumed office as the General Manager, National Productions. Mr. Peter Igho, the new mentor of Chika, was equally another grand master of creative programming like Mr. Iroha.

Mr. Igho's tenure as General Manager National Productions in Lagos left memorable footpints in programme production in NTA. His years marked the golden times of NTA in programming. Mr Igho regionalized the national productions to harness the socio cultural vistas of Nigeria for broadcast and midwifed the evolution of a set of super drama series aired on national television in the early 1980s. Thcsc were; The New Masquerade, produced by Chika Okpala, from the East. The New Village Headmaster, produced by Dejumo Lewis, from the West. The New Samanja, produced by Usman Pategi, from the North and Hotel de Jordan, produced by Joe Ihonde, from Benin. Of course, New Cock Crow at Dawn produced from Jos by Mr. Peter Igho himself.

This college of superlative producers supervised by Peter Igho, engaged in positive competitive productions that kept the nation glued to their TV sets every night on network programming.

Each of these programmes presented the diverse rich cultural settings of the peoples of the zones, while exploring trends and times in their lives. The Village Headmaster x-rayed a typical Yoruba village setting and traditional lives of the natives in the rural Yoruba world of Western Nigeria.

Cock Crow at Dawn was a bit more contemporary with scenes and setting in the rocky hilly highlands of the Plateau region of Nigeria. The New Samanja was a humourous portrayal of the powerful roles of the Regional Sergeant-majors (RSMs) in the regimental lives and duties of soldiers in the military community.

Lifted to the network service, the Masquerade, like the four other regional counterparts acquired the prefix "New", hence the name or title changed to New Masquerade. It was then exclusively entrusted to Chika Okpala as the producer.

It was at this point that the signature tune and graphics were equally changed. Raph Amarabem's "Eddie Kwansa" music track was adopted as the new sound track.

Confirming these radical changes Chika said;

When I took over the production of the New Masquerade in 1984 and the Programme became National Network Programme, the Masquerade was renamed New Masquerade by the general Manager of NTA, National Productions, Mr. Peter Igho. According to Mr Igho, the new name was to take care of all the changes and the new format of the production and to rhyme with the other programmes of national network drama series, namely; The New Village Headmaster, the New Samanja, the new Cock Crow at Dawn.

To make a success of this national responsibility as producer and also the chief Cast of the programmes, he took some measures following the footsteps of his master, James Iroha (OON) when the states were created and they relocated to Imo with Masquerade;

I came down to Enugu with my production crew and anchored at Anambra Broadcasting Service TV (ABS) Channel 50. With permission from NTA headquarters, I negotiated release of Mr. James Iroha, from Imo Broadcasting Service on loan to the New Masquerade on our production days. I also negotiated the re-engagements of Davis Offor, Lizzy Evoeme, Claudius Eke, Christy Essien Igbokwe, Akpeno, Vero Njoku, Romanus Amuta, and Anusionwu Polycarp – Okoro maduekwe, Peter Uwadineke – Mallam Shehu, Tony Akposheri - Zaki, Chinwe Ugwu Aforlene

These were the core casts of the New Masquerade that gripped the land in the 1980s and 1990s. At this point, Chika Chukwunonso Okpala had mutated to a national producer and a national star of repute. He was indeed on the path of fulfilling destiny with acting and stardom with the national TV, the Nigeria Television Authority (NTA).

3.2 ADVENT OF NTA

The Nigeria Television Authority (NTA) is Nigeria's official broadcaster. It is the largest television network in Africa. The station proved true to this rating especially, between the 1980s and the 1990s.

It is common knowledge that radio and television are the major means of broadcasting. Between the two, radio remains the prince and patriarch of the electronic mass media. Television is no doubt younger given the time of its invention in the late 1920s. Its (TV) advent into the Nigerian broadcasting industry came two and half decades after radio.

Unlike radio, which came through the central government, television came through the Chief Jeremiah Obafemi Awolowo led regional government of the Western Region of Nigeria in 1959.

This is to say, Chika was just nine years when television services, through which he excelled into stardom, was born in Nigeria. The bill that brought the Nigeria Broadcasting Corporation (NBC) to life in April 1, 1957, was moved by Hon. D. S. Adegbenro and passed in the Lower House on August 1, 1956. At that time, the country under the British colonial rulers was just three years away from her political independence and operating as a three regional federation. These three regions were in positive stiff competition with one another in all aspects of their lives under the indigenous premiers who were incharge of the regions.

In their tacit competition to establish broadcasting stations in their Regions, Chief Obafemi Awolowo, Premier of the Region established the Western Nigeria Broadcasting Service (WNBS) in 1959. The Eastern Region under Dr. Micheal Iheonukara Okpara, who took over from Dr. Azikiwe as Premier, followed with the Eastern Nigeria Broadcasting service (ENBS) on October 1, 1960. The Broadcasting Company of Northern Nigeria (BCNN) came on air March 15, 1962 established by the Premier of the North, Alhaji Ahmadu Bello.

While Chief Awolowo and his Western region established Television service in 1959, the Central Government came down with National TV service in the land under a five-year management Agency contract with NBC International of the USA in 1962. This marked the birth of the Nigeria Television Service (NTS) which was the forerunner of the Nigeria Television Authority (NTA).

Five years later on March 31, 1967, just four months before the outbreak of the Civil war in the land, the National TV Service was integrated to become the TV arm of the Nigeria Broadcasting Corporation (NBC). The raging war then notwithstanding, television sustained giant strides in flowering colour signals in line with global trends then.

The NBC was also determined to extend to all the state capitals (12 of them then in the country then) there was network of twenty transmitting stations, production centers, and a new national Headquarters to be in Lagos. All these stations throughout the country were linked by a domestic rebroadcast satellite system.

The non-interference of the military government under General Gowon can simply be said to have watered greatly the luxuriant growth of autonomous television broadcasting services in the states. Six years after the war, there were numerous state-owned television stations in major cities across the nation.

The liberty of autonomy enjoyed by the broadcasting institutions in the land under General Gowon ended with the coming of General Olusegun Obasnjo in 1976. On April Fools Day in 1976, he came down with a military fiat that made ownership and control of the broadcasting industry a monopoly of the central government. Board of Governors were set up to run the thriving radio and TV stations taken over from the states by the Federal Government in each state.

Somehow, on a positive note, this cleared the way for the collapse of the old NBC that pioneered broadcasting in the land for over two decades; thus, giving birth to two powerful central television and radio network services under the direct responsibilities of the Federal Government. These are the Nigeria Television Authority (NTA), and the Federal Radio Corporation of Nigeria (FRCN). They officially came into being on April 1, 1977, with Decree No. 24 conferring on the two broadcasting institutions of the NBC, the status of the only officially recognized national radio and television-broadcasting network services in Nigeria. The decree gave the FRCN and NTA the exclusive right for radio/television broadcasting in Nigeria to provide, as a public service (mediums) in the interest of Nigeria, independent and impartial radio/television broadcasting within Nigeria. This decision by government was to restore a sense of national cohesion and propagate common cultural bonds among the ethnic groups in Nigeria through the broadcast of significant local programs.

Nevertheless, the only permanent thing in life, they say, is change.

It came to pass that the dawn of the civilian rule of the second republic in Nigeria in 1979 saw the end of the monopoly of radio and television broadcasting by the Federal government and the return of state ownership of television.

The liberalization of the Nigeria broadcast industry in 1992 saw the coming of the third tier of broadcasting in the land, with the entrance of the private sector that broke the government monopoly for the good of the industry and the people. This indeed, is the background of the broadcasting industry, especially, the National TV, the NTA, the medium Chika dominated as a superstar broadcaster and world-class comic actor of our time.

3.3 THE GOLDEN ERA OF RADIO AND TV

Before Nigeria Television Authority (NTA) was created by the Federal Military Government on April 1, 1977, NTV Channel 6, Aba had existed. It is imperative to underscore the fact that though Aba was not a state capital, which is often preferred for citing of broadcast stations, Aba, being one of the big commercial cities in southern Nigeria could not be ignored by NBC international. It has remained a subject of discussion whether NTA, Aba made James

Iroha, Chief Zebrudaya, and the New Masquerade or vice- versa. What is incontrovertible is that the national stardom and international fame of the trio, did come until NTA, Aba went on network programming.

Aba was a beehive of economic and social activities; spiced with great entertainment shows to unwind. The most popular of which was the famous Mazi Ukonu Club, produced by the NTA, Aba head then, Mazi Anyaogu Elekwachi Ukonu, described by Chika as a foremost entertainer;

First, my respect goes to Mazi Ukonu.

He had a vision and insisted on tangible materials when he came across one. Mazi Ukonu was a foremost entertainer and the producer of the popular Mazi Ukonu's Club on NTA Aba. James Iroha, as a producer, worked under him.

Mazi Ukonu had to bend when James Iroha (OON) insisted that Chika Okpala was a key character in his program "Masquerade" and should be employed by NTA Aba in order to sustain the program and also make him available for rehearsals and productions. Mazi had no choice but to employ me to ensure the existence and continuity of a programmes that kept the nation awake and entertained.

While NTA, ABA was a behemoth of great productions and lively presentations of great programmes and news for the Eastern audience; so were other stations of the NTA across the newly created states, whose works and accomplishments laid a solid foundation for the golden era of both radio and TV services witnessed in the land from the dawn of the 1980s through the 1990s. This was certainly Chika Chukwunonso Okpala times. On March 31, 2019, a publication by allafrica.com corroborates the above assertion;

> *"The 80s and 90s were one of the best TV eras in the history of Nigeria. The period was marked with riveting and captivating soap operas played by indelible characters. From The New Masquerade to Behind the Clouds, these actors evoked nostalgia whenever their names are mentioned. How many of them . . . (indefatigable) Chika Okpala, the veteran TV actor played the lead character Chief Zebrudaya in ''The New Masquerade'. His comedic manner of speaking tinged with correct grammar made him a lovable actor. That character would later cling to him like a second skin, such that whether he is in character or not, the widely held opinion of him is retained as top-of-the-mind. Though he has played other roles in different sitcoms, none has been as nostalgic as the 1980s sitcom, (the New Masquerade. He was honoured with the lifetime achievement award by the Africa Magic Viewers' Choice Awards (AMVCA) in 2017. Recently, he made a cameo appearance in Genevieve Nnaji's Netflix movie, 'LionHeart'.*

One of the major factors that watered and blossomed television in the 1980s and 1990s was the return of broadcast rights to state governments at the dawn of the civilian rule of the second republic (1979–1983). States brought the best of their professionals and great talents to run their radio and TV stations, commonly functioning as two in one stations. This is essentially why James Iroha left NTA, Aba for the newly established Imo Broadcasting Corporation (IBC), Owerri, in 1978.

His exit, especially leaving behind his pet programme, The Masquerade, paved the way for the discovery of new talents in Chika Okpala and Davis Offor (Clarus) who took over the scripting and production of the programme.

As the IBC, established by the first civilian Governor of Imo State, Chief Sam Onunaka Mbakwe was rising in the state, so was Chief Jim Ifeanyichukwu Nwobodo, first Governor of Anambra state then, with an even bigger powerful television arm of the old ECBS, renamed Anambra Broadcasting Service (ABS). This was the famous ATV Channel 50, transmitting on UHF and ranked the best and greatest in Africa in those early days of its birth.

The teaming listeners of the IBC then were awed with the eternally famous weekly drama programme entitled; Ojemba, produced and anchored by Chijoke Abagwe.

Equally, ATV Channel 50 was bubbling with glorious programmes and shows as well as newscasters and presenters with edifying voices and skills like immortal Chuzy Iboko aka Mr. C, Innocent Aniebue, alias Uncle Dickson, veterans like Nworah Asika and Pete Edochie, Igbo newscaster, Chukwuma Ogbonna,

Paddy Ekeh, Walter Eneorah and other great on-air male personalities.

The women were not left out; amazon music maestro and Nollywood star, Onyeka Owenu, Nelly Uchendu, emerged from there. Scintillating presenter like Rosemary Azinge, Lovett Orji, Blessing Akuabata Nwangwu (Igbo), and many other on air personalities that set the airwaves alight to the eternal joy of the audience.

Beyond the news and musicals were series of drama productions both in Igbo and English. Not to be forgotten in a hurry, the weekly, Beyond the Realm, produced by Uzo Amadi and The Mazi Mpirimpi Show. In NTA Channel 8, Enugu, there were other sitcoms that kept the people glued like the famous Ichoku, an Igbo/English drama, inspired by the advent of the whiteman (colonial master) to a typical African setting, with the attendant communication challenge, arising from the whiteman's language and the people's vernacular. The lead character of Ichoku was Lamaji Ugorji, who played the interpreter to the whiteman.

In neighbouring Rivers State, under Medford Okilo, Radio Rivers FM stereo was populated by an array of magnificent on air personalities like Mablas Macaulay Akpoloma (Jnr.), the Reggae whiz kid, Victor Gburugbo, Ken Ekperi, Mike Tokuh, Mike Okiri, who later went into music and released popular didactic hit track, Time Na Money, Florence Ekiye, Bina Koin and others. This TV arm of this state competed favourably with the federal NTA, Port Harcourt. Indeed, across the 19 states of the country, East and West, North and South, state owned broadcasting stations competed with Radio Nigeria and NTA in the art and science of broadcasting.

On December 31, 1983, Major General Muhammadu Buhari and his strong deputy, Brigadier General Tunde Idiagbon, overthrew the second republic civilian government in a military coup. The military government abolished Radio Nigeria's MW/AM stations in the states and handed them over their transmitters to their host states. Though, FRCN and NTA were spared the proscription hammer, they however, experienced operational reorganization, staff and management rationalization to reposition them for optimal performances that gave vent to the golden era of radio and television in Nigeria.

Recall the Super 5 Soap Operas of the New Masquerade, The New Village Headmaster, The New Samanja and Cock Crow at Dawn on NTA Network programming headed by the Executive Producer, Mr. Peter Igho, General Manager, NTA National Productions in Lagos.

The significance of the network programme opportunities cannot be overemphasized because it took regional heroes like Chika Okpala to national and international stardom.

In the Village Headmaster, apart from the producer, Dejumo Lewis, who also played a role in the drama, the star-studded cast had

Femi Robison, the first to play the role of the Village Headmaster; who was succeeded in the role by Ted Mukoro and later, Justice Esiri eternalized himself with the character.

For the New Cock Crow at Dawn, whose scenic vistas and powerful sound track produced by one of Nigeria's iconic soul and country music maestro, Bongos Ikwue, the soap opera was equally star- studded, with Ene Oloja, who played Zamaye, and Sadiq Daba who played the role of Bitrus. Sadiq was a renowned presenter producer who proved a versatile actor and thus a regular feature in most of the 1980s and 90s soap operas such as 'Behind the Cloud', 'A Place Like Home' before emerging one of the superstars of the Nollywood.

Still in the 80s, Behind the Cloud, produced by the ubiquitous Peter Igho, revelaed the likes of Zack Amata Zack, who played Chief Okonzua (Papa Efe), the father of Nosa, played by MacArthur Fom, with Franca Brown as Nosa's mother.

Another glamourous, memorable and highly entertaining TV series of the 80s was late Ken Saro Wiwa's Basi and Company, coming from at ATV Channel 50 studios, Enugu. The main Casts were Basi (Mr. B) played by Albert Egbe before Zulu Adigwe took over the role, The cynosure of the show was the flamboyant madam de madam, played by the vivacious Aso Douglas.

There was also Laolu Ogunniyi's Wind against My Soul that had veteran actress, Ajai-Lycett (OON) and the extraordinary late Sam Loco Efe.

The era brought The Second Chance to the viewers, with Madam Kofo, and her stylish gele played by veteran actress, Abiola Atanda. She also featured in other productions such as 'Mirror in the Sun which had Olu Jacobs. There was Zeb Ejiro's Ripples, which featured Chief Alex Usifo, a man with deep rumbling authoritative voice.

At this time in the East, the bestseller and novel, Things Fall Apart by Chinua Achebe was adapted for TV production, as a project of NTA Zone C, led by NTA, Enugu Station. It was an Igbo langauge adaptation, making it the 49th language translation of the book. The 15-episode film entitled, Okonkwo Dike Ukwu Kporo was adapted by Chidi Aneke and others, while Charles Ugwu was the producer. The main cast, Okonkwo was played by Charles Oguejiofor, Obierika was played by Agunwa Nwokabia, and Okpani Nkama Jnr. made his TV debut Middle way into the production of the film in Igbo language, NTA national management decided to change the language to English, which led to a whirl of controversy. The argument that the production was already too far gone and that the work should be subtitled in English, especially as the novelist, Chinua Achebe, had assented to the Igbo production, was not accepted. This controversy brought disenchantment to many artistes especially the major character led by Charles Oguejiofor. Even when the English production cast were paid better, the major stars in the Igbo version refused to join. This was purely on patriotic whims and Igbo sentiments. When NTA Zone C management refused to suspend the production of the English version and went ahead to solicit and got sponsorship from Chief Ilodibe, CEO, Ekene Dili Chukwu Transport Company, the English production was taken to NTA Zone B in Benin.

This was how **Chief Pete Edochie,** who was already a well-known on-air Radio personality with the ABS and many other stars, were drafted into the film. Edochie, not only asserted himself with the heroic role of Okonkwo, he also broke into national and global prominence when the film hit the screen on the NTA national service in 1986.

In a 2021 online article entitled "The Golden Days of the NTA," Douglas Ogbankwa made these summations on the epic production and Pete Edochie's role as the heroic Okonkwo:

"Okonkwo in Things Fall Apart was the character that beamed Pete Edochie to the world. A younger Edochie interpreted the role with so much conviction in the film adaptation of Chinua Achebe's Things Fall Apart that when he finally moved on to other productions, he was still referred to as 'Okonkwo'.

Well before the production of Things Fall Apart came to NTA, Benin, the station was already the rave among viewers in

Bendel and parts of the south west with **Hotel De Jordan,** a satire that mocked Nigeria's greedy ruling class and the sycophants who urge them on. It had such hilarious characters as grandiloquent Bob Allan played by Richard Idubor, sycophantic characters were Idemudia and Kokori played by Agbonifo Enaruna and David Ariyo, both servants of Chief Ajas played by.**Sam Osamede**

The above drama series on TV nurtured talents, mentored/trained producer and laid the solid foundation for Nollywood. In the early 1990s, multiple award-winning Amaka Igwe, created the sitcom Checkmate, an intriguing story family heritage, unscrupulous business practices, and love tangle. The soap featured Richard Mofe-Damijo (RMD), Ego Boyo, and Uche Obi Osotule, who played a house girl. On the heels of Checkmate came Living In Bondage, a captivating two-part drama thriller, written by Kenneth Nnebue and Okechukwu Ogunjiofor, and directed by Chris Obi Rapu. Many of the casts were already well known like Francis Agu, Bob Manuel Udokwu, Kenneth Okonkwo and Kanayo O Kanayo; and the drama broke new grounds in video production so much, that it heralded the arrival of the Nollywood revolution.

Beyond dramas and soaps, all other aspects of broadcasting – talkshow, news, sports, documentary had great leap during the era, and were equally gripping as soaps. For instance, the sensational Sunday 9pm Newsline, with the duo of Patrick Oke and Yinka Craig, two professionally trained veteran presenters, was on network programme. Frank Olize later took over the news magazine from the duo.

Although he lacked the phonetic finesse of the past presenters, his witty sense of humour and down-right nature endeared him to the viewers and made Newsline, once again, the "Sunday, Sunday" tonic as proclaimed by Frank Olize himself. Undoubtedly, NTA was training ground for most broadcasters and were mentored by the legendary presenter, Segun Olusola, with Shola Omole, John Momoh, who now owns Channels Television, Cyril Stober, the ageless horse, Kalu Otisi and many more.

For glamour ladies of the NTA, we had Ronke Ayuba, the smiling amiable presenter, scintillating Siene Allwell-Brown,

Tokunboh Ajayi, Ruth Benamaisia-Opia and much later, prolific writer Eugenia Abu and others.

From the world of news reporting were; sensational Chris Anyanwu with Abike Dabiri, both veered off into politics and made a huge success of the adventure. Chris now owns a radio station in Owerri.

Other stars of the NTA golden era included such names as Jennifer Anyiam Osigwe, Moju Makunjuola. Augusta Maduegbuna. The men included Segu Aderiyi, Mathew Otaliki, Emma Okondo, with Ben Orji, Manasara Iloh, Akinloye Oyebanji, Paul Ogazi, and Yakubu Ibn Mohammed, who equally rose to be appointed DG, NTA.

With advancement in techonolgy, NTA's era of glory and grandeur came under threat from satellite cable revolution and social media incursion into personalized reportage and online realtime broadcasting on platforms like facebook twitter (now X), and later Instagram. With the deepening mismanagement of public institutions, occasioned by omens of bad governance across federal and state levels, government- owned stations could not compete and yielded to digital technological trends.

3.4 LIFE AFTER NTA & THE BIRTH OF THE ZODIAK BRAINS

By the policy on retirement for public servant, you either attain the statutory retirement age of 35 years in service from the date of employment or you attain the biological age of 60 years from the date of birth. For Chief Chika Chukwunonso Okpala, who joined the service of the NTA, Aba in 1977, his retirement would have been in 2012, if based on length of service or 2010 when he would have attained the mandatory age of 60 yrs for retirement. But this was not the case. Chika voluntarily bowed out of service from NTA, long before both dates, to establish Zodiak Brains Films Ltd, Enugu in 1991. Though 14 years at NTA may be considered a short time, Chika will no doubt beat his chest, like the biblicial Paul, the Apostle, saying; "I have fought a good fight; I have finished my course, I have kept the faith".

His stage performances and production of superlative drama and general entertainment programmes that brought joy, life and laughter to millions across the land, beyond the shores of Africa; and over the Atlantic through the NTA is engraved in our mind and soul forever. Chika's departure from NTA, a medium that brought him fame, glory and global appeal, reinforced the Nigerian aphorism in pidgin English, which aptly captures this interminable circle of civil service career thus; soja go, soja come, barracks remain.

Nonetheless, retirement in whatever form it occurs, presents a different set of challenges and expectations which demands a re-evaluation of the journey ahead. So, for Chika Okpala to have successfully ran the race of public service with the NTA and bowed out when he chose to, strong, hale and hearty, to face his fate in the private sector without those common incidentals that truncate fulfillment of service years, is indeed a mission fulfilled. Chika accomplished his own earthly assignment by nurturing The New Masquerade from a mere drama series into a phenomenon that is incontrovertibly, one of the foundational pillars in the evolution of Nigeria's indigenous film Industry, Nollywood. Not given to complex rhetoric, Chika simply declared;

> *When I look back at my fame represented by a litany of Awards (over one hundred and fifty), crowned with the Federal Government's Awards of the Prestigious Member of the Order of the Niger [MON} and Member of the Order of the Federal Republic of Nigeria [MFR} I feel fulfilled. I have three chieftaincy titles, one from Nnobi, Anambra State, one from Mbaise, Imo State and one from Aba, Abia State. I give thanks to The Almighty God for all the achievements and long life.*

For multi-talented Chika, who had huge appetite for creativity and entrepreneurship, early retirement in sound health opened a new chapter of possibilities. The enormous goodwill, long chain of contact and global experience garnered over the years, becames an asset to explore in entrepreneurship, consultancy and even political adventure. Of course, Chika Okpala settled for his first love – acting, script, production and founded Zodiak Brains Films Ltd in Enugu. In his words;

> *I established and incorporated a state of the art company, Zodiak Brains Films Ltd to carry on with movie productions and public relations, marketing and general promotions consultancy in 1990. My study of Mass Communication afforded me the practice of the above professions.*

This brainchild of Chika's entrepreneurial spirit was commissioned into public use by the former Governor of Enugu state, Dr. Okwesilieze Nwodo, in 1991. Zodiak Brains offered a wide range of services such as; training of budding artistes in acting, script writing, role playing/character moulding, exposure to professional crew management, costume/wardrobe management, make-up, and inculcation of the ethics of professionalism in audio-visual productions. He passionately recalled;

> *My ultimate aim in founding the Zodiak Brains Films Ltd is to develop a niche that shall be seen as a center for information, training and development in the media and the entertainment industry. On the other hand, my goal is to run a center of excellence where human capacity is developed for public, private and NGO institutions; as a change agent for sustainable socio-economic development. We stick to this view by turning out writers of comedy stuff, artiste's development and artiste managers. This is evident in our new productions such as; "Ejiri mara Igbo," "Ahuike dimkpa," "Chairman and Sons," Mmekpa Ahu," "Silent cries" etc. There are over 500 advert/commercial productions on television, over 700 audio commercial productions on radio, developed, written and produced in Zodiak Brains Films Ltd.*

Beyond running Zodiak Brains Films Ltd, Chika attests that he was equally engaged in other related activities since his exit from NTA;

> *Since year 2007, the New Masquerade stopped running on Television, I have occupied my time with production of television commercials and Nollywood shows. I have also given my time to the management and running of Actors Guild of Nigeria Elders Forum, Enugu State Chapter. I still take part in movie productions and will continue. The most important thing about acting is that the older you*

> *become, the more you have matured roles to play in movies. I have been involved in so many Nollywood films that do not offend my conscience. The New Masquerade had always stood against obscene Nollywood productions, especially those that contain offensive acts.*

As an enterprise, Chika equally exploited to the fullest the idea of New Masquerade on stage and available in audio and video tapes. The goodwill element and public acceptability of the show is such that has held out opportunities and patronage for Chika, the ubiquitous "Chief His Royal Palm wine powerless "who are retire from NTA but are not tired on stage." He chipped in mirthfully while revealing that;

For about a decade, the Federal Government of Nigeria always involved the New Masquerade Troupe in National Celebrations. The audience will always watch-out for the New Masquerade Troupe performance, as we will be slated to perform last as the climax of entertainment in the celebrations. There also have been several invitations for stage performances in Europe and America powered by Nigerians in Diaspora. In America, we have performed about twelve times in different states of the USA. In England, we have also performed up to ten times. Down here in Africa, the New Masquerade was always engaged to perform in Cameroon, Sierra Leone, Liberia and the Gambia.

PART FOUR

MARRIAGE, WORK & FURTHER EDUCATION

4.1 Marriage
4.2 His Odyssey for a Spouse
4.3 Tertiary Education
4.4 Managing Fame and Marriage
4.5 His Wife, His Wand of Success
4.6 His Good, Bad and Ugly Times

4.1 MARRIAGE

Before embarking on his long trek through tertiary Institutions in quest of higher academic status as a broadcaster, Chika Chukwunonso Okpala had come of age for marriage. This is a very crucial stage in the life of a young adult. Contrary to the tenets of the Western world view on marriage institution, in Africa, it is one of the compulsory rites of passage. The life of a typical African is essentially unfulfilled without marriage which inevitably comes with its accompanying fruits of the womb. The issues of sustenance of family name and genealogy constitute the core essence of marriage to an African.

In Igboland, the saying; iluta nwanyi - literarily meaning taking a wife, holds such sacred pride of place that when one comes of age without getting married, he is not only seen as spiritually, psychologically and socially incomplete, but also considered an efulefu – the worthless one. The craving for a wife came to young Chika in 1981. As a thorough-bred Igbo son, Chika would not take such major step in life without the consent of Chief Daniel Okpala, his father and his Umu Nna, family elders; for the simpe reason that: otu onye anaghi alu nwanyi, meaning; **One man does not contract marriage**.

Therefore, the prospective husband and wife, curiously, had little or no voice in the matter. Parents indulged in matchmaking their children. In a few cases, where the young adult is courageous enough to finds a heartthrob for his/herself, parental consent is a must for such whimsical intentions to materialize into marriage. Apart from being insensitive to the feelings of their sons or daughters involved, mundane considerations have often ruled the motives of these parents especially, the less economically privileged ones.

Interestingly, Chika was a typical victim of this situation in his bid to take a wife and settle down. While his rising fame as an actor and popular TV personality, Chief Zebrudaya, made him one of the most eligible bachelor, his strong-willed father, Chief Daniel Okpala, still had his way in the choice of Chika's wife. Chika leaves us here with this interesting testimonial on his odyssey to choosing a wife to marry.

4.2 HIS ODYSSEY FOR A SPOUSE

In 1981, young Chika sought the consent of his parents to get married, ignoring his "army of lady acquaintances", as he often called. Interestingly, this quest for consent turned into a thrilling story as he revealed in this interactive session:

Q: Now Chief, typical of thespians, we learnt your present wife was not the first woman you settled with in your journey into marriage, please, can you share with us what really happened?

ZB: *Well, even before the first marriage with late Edith, I had taken home as many as about seventy girls I wanted to marry in different occasions to show my parents for their consent and blessing. This is because anywhere I went to perform I see people who wanted to get closer to me and they looked good. But I would always say to each of them don't worry we will marry but I had to get home to clear with my parents. And I will take the person home to show my parents. But none of these clicked. It got to a point that when my father sees me driving home with a lady in my car. . . I was driving a Beetle car then, he will quickly go and get his agbu (the palm tree climbing rope) and his knife and put on his raffia cap to leave the house. When I say to him, 'Dad, I came for a serious discussion to acquaint you with my new acquaintance, he will tell me the goats at the back yard have been crying since morning and he was in a hurry to go fetch palm fronds for them before nightfall. He will hurriedly leave, abandoning us for a long wait. Even when he was done with his mission out there he will not come home. He will either go to visit a friend or branch into a (tombolikwor) palm wine joint and stay to while away time just to avoid any marriage discussion with me. And I will not want to sleep over because I must go to work the next day, I will grudgingly embark on a late night drive back to Aba from Nnobi On one occasion when I was at Jos doing Cock Crow at Dawn, I came back with someone, a Hausa girl to show him, he looked at me for a while and said; "you mean you left the whole of Igbo land and did not see any girl here to marry and you want to put me to awusa . . . tufiaaaa! You didn't see me! (Laughter). How can your children be going to see their grandparents in case you don't have money to fly or charter a vehicle to take them?*

Thoroughly dispirited and embarrassed, I grudgingly stuttered "Dad, I will have money . . . I will get money . . . And he angrily retorted, "enhee! You will get money? Ok! Please, when you have this kind of ladies again don't come to me, don't call me!"

The next time actually came when I went for an NTA workshop in Lagos. One young Yoruba lady was so close to me and so liked me and seemed to have wanted me at all cost. So, I said to her, look I don't want to mess up my life, all I wanted was to find a girl to marry. She said aah aah! Marriage, we can marry, I be omo Yoruba, you be omo Ibo, we can marry, there's no problem there. I said fine, no problem, can you teach me Yoruba? And she said, why not, so long as you teach me Igbo. And I said that won't be a problem at all. So, I came home with her one day; that one was so down to earth, before you know it she had taken broom and swept the whole place goat messed up, the whole compound was kept neat. She went to my mother's room swept and packed it well, came to the palour scrubbed it with water and everywhere was neat. She was that neat and my mother developed likeness for her, but we spent just two nights. Still, that one like many others I came home to present didn't click with my father. Chief Daniel continued in his ways against the army of acquaintances I came home with to seek his consent and blessing for marriage. Each time he sees me coming with a lady he will go for his agbu and disappear.

So, one day I said to him, 'Daddy, what is the matter? Why are you doing this to me? Do you know you are disgracing me? He said no, he was not. 'If you want to marry, the day you are ready let me know'. And I said, 'Ok, I want to marry now, do you have anyone for me? Who is she?' Delightfully, he said; 'Ehnee . . . now you're talking! Now, you're coming home, thank God for this. There's this friend, Ogbuefi Nnayelugo, the titled one, there's a girl in his compound, I learnt the girl's father is in Chad . . .'

I said; 'Ehnee, so I will now go to Chad to get married?'

He said 'No, calm down now . . . yes, the father of the girl is in Chad, but if you're serious you want to marry her, we can ask Nnanyelugo to send a message to his brother, the father of the girl, he doesn't even need to be home since the brother, Nnanyelugo is at home". I said ok, 'where is the lady? I want to see her, I won't marry anyone of those they cover from head to toe and they say come and choose, I want to see this one, if I like her that's fine. He said that one is not a problem, 'but are you prepared to go to Enugu tomorrow? The young girl is working in Enugu. I said that's Ok, let me have the address? My father quickly rode on his bicycle to get the address from Nnanyelugo. The next morning, I drove to Enugu, went to the Chief Ekwueme street address I was given. In the compound I was directed to, they lived upstairs. As God would have it, I met one Permanent Secretary who happens to be a town's man from Nnobi living opposite the flat the lady (my wife) lived. I told the man who I was looking for, he said why not see me in my office tomorrow at Ministry of Finance I did the next morning and he told me that he employed Christiana, the lady I was looking for, that she works at the Federal Pay Office, Zik Avenue, Uwani. I drove to the Federal Pay Office, Uwani and met the boss. He was so excited and called the workers to come and see Chief Zebrudaya Okoroigwe Nwogbo alias 4.30 in his office. I told him my mission and he said I should wait, for the girl I was asking for was out on an assignment. Well, although I had in mind to leave for Jos possibly that day, but I had no choice than to wait. So, I sat in his office and waited. Hour after, the lady I came for came back and her colleagues told her someone, a big fish she caught was waiting for her in their boss's office.

Their boss then sent for her and she came in, and he said to her this man came for you and he has a good proposal, please, listen to him.

Apparently, what happened that day makes me suspect somebody must have briefed her from home, perhaps to accept my proposal. The boss kindly excused us to go and talk. We went out and talked. I told her my name is Chika Okpala, people know me as Chief Zebrudaya Okoroigwe Nwogbo, alias 4.30. I am on the Cock Crow at Dawn project in Jos. So, I came down all the way from Jos to see you. My parents have already started embarrassing me about marriage. So, the long and short of this visit is that my parents said I should come and see you, to know whether you can marry me and I can marry you. What do you say?

She didn't answer me rather she started drawing figure three on the ground with her foot. "Aah aah! What do you say now?" I asked quite anxious. She didn't talk. Why are you drawing three, I am serious o, do you say we should come, with my parents? Remember I am not home, I am not at Aba, I am at Jos, and we should be fast to conclude all these things. She didn't know what to say. Give me an answer now! Do you say we should come? I asked again with a tinge of impatience.

She then said 'eeh, you people can come.' And I said are you sure? She firmly replied; 'yes! You people can come.'

I thanked her and went back and thanked the boss and told him we will follow up at home. When I got home, I told my parents that I have seen the lady, she is ok, pretty and presentable, but she was busy drawing three, three, three on the ground. I need somebody who can look at me and we talk. Somebody I can discuss issues with, not someone I would be talking to and she would be looking the other way. I don't need a shy person. My mother then emphatically said; Chika what you need is a shy person. (Laughter) that is the person you need, you don't need fire-fire, you need ice water. . .

I said yes she looks ice water mom, just that this three-three-three she is drawing when I am talking to her . . . Me I don't know, supposing we go out and I am on the microphone and people want to hear my wife and she is a shy one, can she talk to the microphone?

Persistently, my mother said "Chika nwam, what you need is ice water, you're hot, what you need is somebody to cool you down." I said ok! 'In that case do you approve that? Enthusiastically they said yes . . . yes! Let's go ahead. My father added, "don't go and bring ofe manu (referring to the Yoruba lady), or Amina (referring to the Hausa lady) here to me again o!" I promised I wouldn't do that and made up my mind to settle with this one. The next day on my way to Jos, I stopped by at Enugu for her to take me to the uncle she was living with at Chief Ekwueme street. We met and the man heartily welcomed me to his house and was happy at my marriage proposal.

He said the father was in Chad, but that was not a challenge. Later my father fixed a date for the first knocking on the door. This was the first visit to furnish intention of marriage to the bride's parents according to Igbo marriage rites. After that every other rite was duly followed and fulfilled and the marriage consummated between us with a church wedding at Our Lady of Lourdes Catholic Church, Aba in 1981.

Today, that shy young woman holds a Master's Degree in Business Management. She had three children (two girls and a boy) for me - Adora, Afam and Ogechukwu. We lost Adora at 16 years. Bless her soul.

The surviving ones; Afam, had his first degree in computer science from NnamdiAjkiwe University, Awka, Anambra State and had a Master's Degree from Belarus University, Belarus, Russia. Ogechukwu is also a graduate of Anambra State University, Uli. They are both working and married with children. This ended my escapades with about seventy girls in quest of just one to marry (Laughter).

Q: *Chief! Seventy Inyoms (ladies) for one! . . . You alone! Dimkpa k 'ibu! (Up roar of laughter again) Ok, let's come to the first marriage, we learnt it was short-lived. What happened?*

ZB: *Yes! Her name was Edith from Ibeku, Umuahia. I met her during one of my shows at Umuahia which she attended. She came in the company of one Mr. Ogbonna who had been an old acquaintance while in Enugu. At the end of the show, people were thronging to the back stage to shake hands and take photographs with us while we were changing clothes. So, while I was exchanging pleasantries with Dee Ogbonna as we called Mr. Ogbonna, Edith was eyeing me too much which made Mr. Ogbonna to jocularly ask her; 'the way you are eyeing Chief Zebrudaya, would you want to marry this old man?' We all laughed and you know women, Edith said to him; 'why are you asking me, must you know who I want to marry?' And Dee Ogbonna replied; 'don't worry, I know him very well, after the show I will properly introduce you to him'.*

And that's what happened. So I told her that as she can see I was with my troupe, and cannot spare much time to chat with her, why don't you pay me a visit at Aba, that I lived at 31 Park Road, Aba, if you want to come. And so, she came visiting. By then, I didn't know what she was doing for a living. It was when we got talking that she told me she finished at Alvan Ikoku College of Education then and was a teacher at Ibeku High School, Umuahia. She said she intended to go further fi there's fund, but as at the time her mother was catering for five of them in the house. They had lost their father long time ago. She alone was sponsoring the younger brother who was in a University in South Africa.

Q: So, what did you tell her?

ZB: *Well, I told her that was fine. As for me, I had not gone to any higher institution. As God would have it, I was just exploiting my talent in acting and the fame was just coming small small. She said "Noo! The fame was not coming small oo! It was already beyond the state and all over the place and across Nigeria."*

And I said I thanked God for that. I did not want to take her to any hotel, I told her that I had yam, I had garri, but the problem is that I didn't have soup can she go and prepare soup for me? She said why not, am I not a woman? So she went and prepared one of those delicacies of Umuahia, ofe achara and okazi which was alien to me as a full blooded Nnobi, Anambra man. You know we are always talking of ofe onugbu, ofe ora etc. So, I tested variety that day and they were quite testy.

She made the two types of soup (Okazi and Achara) and stored in the refrigerator for me. The discussion was getting quite interesting. Two days after the first, visit she came back to Aba. That was how the journey to marriage began.

Q: Was the marriage properly formalized?

ZB: *Yes! You know, one man does not contract marriage in Igbo land. So, I had to meet my parents and informed them that I had found somebody to marry. I confessed to them that the lady was down to earth, and had cooked for me o and her cooking was good. I told them she was a teacher in a secondary school and speaks well. So, we had to meet her people and formalized things and by December that year, 1979 we got married.*

Q: So what happened to the marriage that you went into escapades bringing seventy other girls to your parents for blessing to marry?

ZB: *Well, that is one of the saddest experiences I had in life. Her sudden death barely a month after our marriage was quit devastating. As I said earlier, we got married in December 1979 and in January 1980, the New Masquerade had a show in Calabar and I went with the troupe leaving her hale and hearty at her residence in Ibeku High School, Umuahia. We came back two days after to Aba and here was the principal of her school, Ibeku High School, who drove all the way to Aba to invite me to follow him immediately to the School. It was a curious invitation and I followed him without questions. On our arrival at the school compound, the entire school had assembled at her house. Edith taught Mathematics and Physics. It was then I began to have a hunch that something awful must have happened. From the school compound I was then taken to the hospital, Queen Elizabeth Hospital, Umuahia where she was still on her hospital death bed. After heavy depression and confusion, I ordered the hospital to take her to the morgue, while I went home to my people and her people for her burial later. Up till date I still don't have a reasonable explanation as to what led to her death. It was a terrible tragedy. Her death affected me so badly. It was just barely a month into our marriage, this is given the fact that we married in December and she died in January.*

In spite of his escapades afterwards, Edith's early demise in their marriage has remained a lingering mystery and sad experience for Chika. Even with the eternity of years that has passed since her painful exit. Chika remembers her with profound sense of sadness and loss.

Well, life is a great ocean flowing endlessly with the run of time and seasons for all things under heavens. Every human born into life is born to swim and sink at his/her destined time in the turbulence of this deep and vast ocean (life). So is marriage a tributary of the ocean of life. There's no knowing how deep or shallow it is until one steps into it. There's equally no knowing where, when and how the lurking hippos and crocs in the river of marriage will leash its killer attacks on the couple for the ultimate end of the life union. Some survive the perils and swim far, while some sink few years into the swim. For some like Chika and his late Edith, the crocs strike at the starting shore of the marriage swim, thus bringing the ultimate end of marriage.

4.3 TERTIARY EDUCATION

In those days, when Chika was still in service, academic qualification was not a major prerequisite for promotion or career progression in civil service. For this, workers were not expected to combine their work with higher academic pursuits in schools. Those who enrolled in schools for higher academic learning were doing so for their personal self-advancement and satisfaction than for their career. In fact, they run the risk of obtaining a higher certification above their bosses which could elicit envy in the workplace. However, this policy changed with time allowing workers pursue higher academic qualifications to advance in service. Such academic pursuit was best suited for part time bases to ensure it did not affect the job and undermine service. This gave Chika room to begin the move to improve his academic qualifications. Naturally, the discipline had to be in his line of service at NTA and mass communication came handy, as Chika explained;

> *Although I was deeply involved in drama productions especially comedy, I was madly in love with journalism, reporting from different parts of the world. When I inquired of the surest course to become correspondent / Journalist, the answer I got was Mass Communication.*
>
> *So I went in for Diploma in Mass Communication to Master's Degree in Mass communication and then to Master's Degree in Business Admin.*

This certificate acquisition followed Chika's familiar twists and turns path to success. It began far back in 1983 shortly after his return to NTA, Aba from his national assignment of taking up the production of the New Masquerade in Lagos.

One Dr. Nnanna Ukaegbu, who was the Proprietor of one of those private universities in the East then, offered him and his colleague, Davis Offor, a grant to study in his school named; TEDEM (Imo Tech. University) at Imerienwe, Owerri. They began with remedial courses that were to enable them qualify for degree programme in Theatre Arts. But this programme was truncated by the coming of Generals Muhammadu Buhari and Tunde Idiagbon to power. Their sweeping proscription of private schools including tertiary institutions led to the closure of the TEDEM University where they were running their remedial courses.

His next destination for his higher academic pursuit was the University of Nigeria, Nsukka (UNN). It was in this premier institution that he began his quest to study mass communication. This was between 1989 and 1991. First, he bagged a diploma in mass communication at UNN. Next, he joined the Mature Student Programme (MSP) of Enugu State University of Technology (ESUT) for a Bachelor's Degree (B.Sc) in mass communication. This ran from 1989 to 1996.

There, at the same Faculty of Social Sciences, Chika went ahead to study and acquire a second degree in mass communication from year 2000 to 2004. He then crowned this academic glory with another Master's Degree in Business Administration (MBA), this time, from the National Open University of Nigeria (NOUN) between 2012 and 2017.

As a famous superstar, Chika was by all means an executive student. And like a golden fish that had no hiding place, he knew all eyes were on him and given his humble and easy going ways, he had no problem conforming to the expected humility, discipline, good conduct and comportment demanded of students by the institution. He provided some form of leadership, emerging as President of the

MSP in his course during his years of study. He endured with patience some unavoidable high-handedness and the demi-god attitude of some university teachers over their students.

4.4 MANAGING FAME AND MARRIAGE

Marriage, fame and power rarely co-exist harmoniously in a sentence. Amongst celebrities, especially thespians, music artistes, sports stars and other highly creative geniuses, fame brings social and financial power resulting in drugs, multiple sex partners, pride and other vices. In the West, there was Elizabeth Taylor, ranked one of the prettiest actresses to grace the tubes; her escapades with men led to eight failed marriages and four children. In recent history, Michael Jackson was the world's greatest pop singer; but he struggled with marital issues and raising his own family, before his sad end in a controversy of performance enhancing drug abuse.

Even in Africa, where marital status and raising nucleus family remain crucial to the people, a life of easy virtue has proven to be an Achilles' heel for our famous thespians/stars.

A reference case is that of Nigeria's **Majekodunmi Fasheke** aka **Majek Fashek,** nick named the rain maker for the historic album, featuring the hit track, '*Send down the Rain*' in 1988. Painfully, consistent use of drugs wrecked his successful music career and crashed his marriage leading to his untimely death at age of 57.

South African superstars, **Miriam Zenzile Makeba** aka **Mama Africa** and **Brenda Nokuzola Fassie,** suffered similar fate. Regarded as one of the most powerful female vocalists out of Africa to rule the world of music, both iconic singers and anti- Apartheid activists wrestled with multiple marriages, drugs and a laissez faire lifestyle

What about the 'elegant stallion' of the Nigerian entertainment industry, Onyeka Owenu (MFR)! The sensational broadcaster, singer, and actress is arguably one of the few talented persons to combine, successfully, journalism (broadcasting), an illustrious musical career, and Nollywood stardom. Her litany of awards, hit tracks and box office success which began with a documentary on corruption, titled, '*Squandering of Riches*', is marred by a litany of marital woes and an unenviable relationship. Blunt and frank as ever, she offered, *"I went through it (marriage). It was difficult because I really didn't want my marriage to end, but I couldn't take it anymore, it would have killed me . . ."*

By some Providence, the New Masquerade stars were spared the marriage vs fame crisis. Chief Zebrudaya Okoroigwe Nwogbo – alias 4.30 may be a polygamist on TV, but Chief Chika Okpala is a monogamist, loving husband and caring father to his children. Worthy of note is legendary Christy Uduak Essien Igbokwe (MFR), who played Akpenor, the boisterous Yoruba wife of Prince Jegede Shokoya, in the New Masquerade. Like Onyeka Owenu (MFR), she combined acting and signing, becoming the first female president of the Performing Musicians' Association of Nigeria (PMAN) in 1996. Christy married Edwin Igbokwe and remained a faithful wife, mother of four sons and responsible super star till she passed in 2011.

4.5 HIS WIFE, HIS WAND OF MARRIAGE SUCCESS

After his intriguing odyssey of scanning over 70 ladies for the right spouse to marry, coupled with the harrowing loss of his first wife, a month after wedding, Chief Zebrudaya Okoroigwe Nwogbo alias 4.30, has remained as constant as the northern star with Christy, his one and only wife and mother of his children since 1981. He has weathered the storms of marriage with the daunting challenges of the work as a producer, scriptwriter, director and actor par excellence.

Chika Okpala's grand success in managing fame and family can be attributed to the kind and character of the woman he married. Beyond her professed love and pride for her husband who is a global figure, Christy, Madam Zebrudaya in real life, is a quiet unassuming woman from highly disciplined home.

By her Christian tenets, she is a strong believer that the man is the king in the home and the woman, a helpmate. Dr. Ogbonnaya Frank Jackson, who was his manager and cameraman right from their early days in NTA Channel 6, Aba, attests that; "Madam is the quiet type; she is not the kind that is too suspicious or one that nags over her husband's social affairs. I think she learnt early in their marriage to accept her super star husband's character traits, and the nature of his work. This entails he could be away from the home for weeks on end and even when he is home, she and the kids may still not have his attention because of his tenacity to delivering productions. Chief can keep awake in the studio for days and weeks working on a production. He takes his work very seriously. It is on production you will see that his jovial, easy-going nature has its boundaries and deep shades of seriousness. Madam has long learnt to keep off, thus sustaining the bond of mutual respect and peace between the two"

Frank was not alone in this testimony of the humane and humble nature of Madam Chika Okpala. Leo Spider Osuji, (Udude Nnobi) is Chief Okpala's kinsman who knows the couple individually from their homes. "The wife, let me call her by her native name, 'Omuluzuo', she happens to come from the same kindred with me. We are all kind of related. Omuluzuo is a person who cannot hurt a fly. I don't know, may be because they lived in Cameroon with their father, they acquired a simple lifestyle attitude. They tend to take things as easy as they see it without attaching too much importance to things. Christy Omuluzuo Okpala is a person who knows how to interact with people, takes cognizance of others feelings when she wants to do things. She doesn't make noise but at the same time don't step on her toes." Osuji concluded.

Another major factor that made Chika successful as a rare super star husband and family man is that he is a man who does not joke with his children and their welfare. He plays with them and they are always looking forward to his return after his many duty tours that kept him away from them. He tells me in advance what job he is chasing, where he will be and how long it may take to complete the task.

There is this saying that jealousy is a chronic infirmity without a known cure especially among wives. It is equally a bane of peaceful marriage. Christy understands that marrying a super star whose name tolls the bells is socially herculean, attracting envy, and suspicion stimulating. To deal with it, she shuns gossips and hearsay and tenaciously sticks to believing her man.

Does it also worry her that many think that Ovularia Uredia Nwogbo, her husband's TV wife is the real wife? Christy wondered why she should be, especially as she claerly understands her husband's job in the world of make-believe.

Below are the excerpts of the interview with Christy Okpala, the real wife of Chief Zebrudaya:

Q: Madam, what's your name?

CHRISTY: My name is Christiana Ebele Omunuzuo Okpala

(Nee) Ogbuefi. I am from Umuobi, Nnobi in Idemili South Local Government of Anambra State.

Q: Before we get to know when and how you met your husband, let's know a bit of your background ma?

CHRISTY: The early stage of my life began in Douala, Cameroon where my parents lived and did their business. My father was running a big restaurant in Douala, while my mom traded on ladies wears and sowing materials. I am the (Ada), first daughter and first born of the house with two other siblings. It was there in Cameroon that I started my primary education. However, it was while I was in my primary three that my parents brought us home to Nnobi and left us in the care of my grandmother.

Q: What year was that?

CHRISTY: That was after the war in 1970. I resumed school at Obi Memorial Primary School, Nnobi to complete my primary education before gaining entrance into Girls Secondary school, Nnobi. After my secondary school in 1977, I went to Enugu and got a little Job at the Pay Office of Ministry of Finance. It was here at the Pay office, Enugu that I met him (Chika, her husband) for the first time. He came to the office and was asking to see me. I was staying with my uncle at Chief Ekwueme Street, Uwani, Enugu. My uncle who invited him to come had briefed me of his intentions and so when I saw him in the office and he asked for my hand in marriage, I accepted.

Q: Was this your quick acceptance based on obedience to parental wishes or based on the fact that you liked him when you saw him, what was the chemistry?

CHRISTY: With the appearance and the kind of man he is, so

jovial and playful, and he is down to earth. With the first discussion we had, I said okay, even before he said this is why he came, I accepted him.

Q: Before then, you may have been seeing him on TV . . .
CHRISTY: (Interrupts) Yes! I had seen him twice before then.

Q: Just twice? The Man and Legend of New Masquerade: Zebrudaya

CHRISTY: Yes!

Q: Could this be part of why you fell for him? CHRISTY: Yes! It was.

Q: Okay, that means you accepted him not because your uncle said you should. What other things made you like him?

CHRISTY: As I said, he is a jovial man, down to earth, he is a man of his words, in fact, his appearance appealed to me and I saw him as one who could stay with somebody for life.

Q: You know men are like tigers, big cats with nine lives when they want a girl they may promise her heaven on earth, but when they succeed in getting what they want, often you see them changing. In the case of our man, is this true or is he the same man you met and said yes to his proposal for marriage?

CHRISTY: Yesoo! He is still the same, there's not much difference. He is still the same person. And I thank God for it.

Q: Now, let me ask you this direct question, you know this man is an actor, a super star whose name rings a bell? In most cases there's always this problem of faithfulness in marriage with them, what is the case with Chief Zeby? Do you consider him a womanizer who pretends well to be faithful to you?

CHRISTY: Eehm! I see him as somebody who is straight forward, he is one who is very serious with his job, one who cares less about such frivolities, he travels a lot for his job and I understand what he is doing, when you go out with him you will see crowd of people flocking around him, his fans will practically snatch him away from you. But in all these, I trust him, essentially because he has proved he is a man of his words, who is not into all those things.

Q: Really? But don't you sometimes feel somehow suspicious of him as a woman?

CHRISTY: Well yes! As a woman, I am bound to feel like that, but because he always comes back to explain what he is doing and being one I have come to trust as a man of his words helps a lot to comfort me and kill any suspicion. Besides, what I am after is my joy, not all those rubbish imaginations or what people say.

Q: When you met this man, he was already a very busy man, and on the move with his work and stardom. Did you ever have what can be called a honeymoon, in other words, time for yourselves?

CHRISTY: Yes! We did. As a matter of fact, he normally creates out time for us to be together each time he comes back before moving out again.

Q: Both of you are Catholics, when did you people marry and if you had a church wedding where and in which church?

CHRISTY: We got married in 1981 and wedded at Our Lady of Lourdes Catholic Church, Aba.

Q: When did the children start coming?

CHRISTY: That was in 1982, when we had our first child, Adora, we lost her in 1998. Then second child our first son, Afam

Henry Okpala in 1983, and the third child, our second daughter Ogechukwu Anita Okpala in 1987. On the whole, we had three children.

Q: Well, it's a common fact that no man or woman is perfect, just as no union of marriage is perfect, what would you say are the weaknesses and strengths of your man as a father, husband and man?

CHRISTY: Well, it is true that no man or marriage is perfect, but I can't say this particular thing and that are his weaknesses, because we have been moving on fine. He could be hash and rash if you don't do what is right, be you his wife, child, relative or worker. He has no patience for failure; he believes people must do their jobs no matter what.

Q: Now how do you cope with his reported attitude of holding so tenaciously to his productions that he could be away from home for days or weeks and when he comes back he may run into the studio and spend days on end working on a production without sparing time for anything or anybody else until he is done?

CHRISTY: Well, while that looks like a challenge, it is not to us because we always discuss his itinerary before he sets out for it. Good enough he has this habit of telling me in advance what job he is chasing, where he shall be and would say to me, 'please, mark this date... mark this day o! I will be at so so so place . . . for so so so purpose'. So, with that I will know where he's going and when he's coming back and what he will be doing and avoid interfering.

Q: Great! Now, being his wife means you are equally a global figure yourself, but somehow, not many know about his wife and family. As a matter of fact, many think that Ovularia Uredia Nwogbo, his TV wife is the real wife. So, one wonders if he is busy suppressing and silencing his family from limelight, what is the true situation?

CHRISTY: Aaah noo! He is not suppressing us at all. In any case, that is often the case with most of these super stars. So, his case on this is not anything special and I am not complaining about that . . . am I? (Laughter}

Q: Well, from all indications you are not ma! But does that worry you that his TV wife is the one generally thought to be his real wife?

CHRISTY: Not at all. I do not worry about imaginations that are not true. I am the one with him in reality, so?

Q: It's alright ma! Now, what is your relationship like with the other artistes like Akpenor, when she was alive, Vero Njoku (Ramota) and Ovularia?

CHRISTY: Oooh, very cordial! When they come for their rehearsals and recording and I happen to be around, I relate very well with them, in fact, I feel free with them knowing that they are doing their job. I don't think of any other thing. Lizzy, who is the Ovularia you are talking about, is just like a mother to me . . . that's it!

Q: That's great to hear! Now, after all these years together, if you are taken back to 1981 when he proposed to marry you, would you still have accepted to marry him now you have seen the good, the bad and ugly side of him?

CHRISTY: O' yes! I will of course marry him . . .

Q: The last questions ma'am, what would you precisely remember your husband for and what are your wishes and prayer for him and the children?

CHRISTY: Ooh! I will remember my husband for his hard work and fatherly care for us. He is always there for us, when there's a problem in the house, he's ever there for us, in fact, he is a true father, I just thank God for him . . . he is a complete family man and a very hard working man. As for my prayer and wishes for him, I pray every day that the Lord grants him long life and good health to enjoy the fruits of his hard work and for us to be together for more time here on earth before departing to meet our creator. And for our remaining children, I wish and pray they should all make it in life; that they should emulate their parents and stick to doing the right thing and working hard to succeed in all they do.

After her wedding to Chika Okpala (Chief Zebrudaya) in 1981, she returned to school for higher academic qualifications in the hope of joining the teaching profession. She ran a two-year teachers' training course at the Teachers Training College (TTC) , Aba in 1983. With her Teacher's Grade Two Certificate (TC II), she later proceeded to Ehamufu College of Education, Enugu State in 1985 for a National Certificate in Education (NCE). She then went to University of Nigeria, (UNN), Nsukka, and bagged her first degree in French Language in 1991. After her National Youth Service (NYSC) with the Universal Trust Bank (UTB), Aba, Christy said the Bank retained her and she worked for five years there. While at the UTB, Aba, she enrolled in the distant education programme of the Imo State University (IMSU), Owerri, first, for a Post Graduate Diploma (PGD) in Business Management and then, Master's degree in the same Business Management between year 2000 and 2003. The quiet unassuming deep Catholic faithful lady, Christy Omunuzua Okpala currently teaches French language in Federal Govt College, Enugu.

His Son – Afam Okpala

Q: Afam, please, I want your candid opinion, what manner of man is your father?

AFAM: My father is a very nice man, jovial, accommodating and someone who always wants the best for his children, not just his children, but anyone around him. He is a very lovely Father anyone would wish. To sum it all, he is a very wonderful Father

Q: What is your relationship with him like?

AFAM: Our relationship is a typical Father and Son relationship marked with mutual love and respect. This very father is one who loves to carry his son along in all he does. Our relationship has been so beautiful and wonderful; he never ceases to correct me or give me ideas on how to face life with ease. This makes our relationship so lovely and beautiful. Simply put, his love for me and the family has been awesome.

Q: I see, quite good to hear. What do you like and dislike most about him?

AFAM: Well, I like almost everything about him because he has always been there for us, I like the way he cares for the family, how he takes care of difficult situations when they arise and how he gives and cherishes anyone that comes around him. He has always been a good man and dislike cheating. When you work for him, he never cheats you. This is granting he is very strict essentially because he wants things to be done properly. So, you have to be hard working before you work for him. I like his passion for success.

Well, on the other hand, what I dislike about him is his refusing to join politics, because he is a very good person and loved by the people. I'm 100% sure he is a good leader.

Q: Would you like to be born by such man as father in your next world?

AFAM: Of course, over and over again. He is a company you would love to be with every day. I have learnt a whole lot from him. And all that I learnt from him has been so helpful to me. So, such a man deserves to be around. He is a great man and a legend. My Father, Chief Chika Okpala is so dear to me and I repeat, I would love to be his son over and over again.

Q: I see! You learnt quite a lot from your father and like almost everything about him except his acting and comic prowess. But it seems none of you his surviving children is interested in the acting business as we see of children of his contemporaries in the Industry . . . Is it that the gene failed here or what?

AFAM: (Laughs) Oh no no no! It's not like that. Believe me, that I didn't go into acting early in my life doesn't mean I have no interest, No! The truth is that I was so much focused on Engineering and IT Services, and that made me look the other way. As it's now, I am open to acting because most of my activities are still connected to making people to laugh. You see, genes don't lie and don't fail . . . (laughter).

Q: (Interjects) Anam anu . . . I hear you! We are waiting for your Ijele! (The great Masquerade in Igbo land). (Laughter).

His Daughter – Anita Idume (Mrs)

Q: Yes, madam, tell us what kind of man is your father?

ANITA: He is a modest and God fearing man, very affectionate, comforting, understanding, he makes things look seamless. He always tells me 'there's nothing you can't achieve

if you set your mind in pursuit of it'. His words of affirmation literally motivate me a lot.

Q: How do you relate with him and vice versa as daughter and father?

ANITA: Well, our relationship has been a wonderful one. We've had lots of good times together. Whenever am around we'll have a lot to catch up, he has really thought me a lot and am so proud to have him as my Father.

Q: What do you like and dislike most about him?

ANITA: Hmmm, I just can't think of something that I will categorically say that makes me feel disappointed to have him as a father or dislike him. He has always been there for me and the rest of the family. He's God fearing, he has thought us the word of God. We've prayed together, he is just phenomenal. His exuberance and passion for being a good dad and husband is fascinating. He is such a great man.

Q: Assuming there's a next world, would you like to be born by such man as father?

ANITA: Yes! I would definitely want to be his daughter again if we have the opportunity for a next life.

4.6 HIS GOOD, BAD & UGLY TIMES

It was the Crystal Palace builder in the US, Dr. Robert Schuller, in his profound appraisal of the ups and downs of life that philosophically stated; *"tough times don't last but the tough do . . ." (for) "when the going gets tough, the tough gets going."*

Truly, life generally is like a wave in its up-and-down movement. Life is equally like a checkered hurdle course ran through hostile hilly planes and volatile valleys of the good, the bad and ugly times for the individual. Every man, in his lifetime therefore, experiences his low and high times. It is never an endless run of similitude of bad times and vice versa; it breaks and fluctuates, blowing hot and cold on the individual at unpredictable intervals in the run of his years. It all depends on one's stamina and the grace of God who actually predetermines the mileages - being the number of years every individual lives here on earth, and the milestones being the individual's accomplishments in his/her journey through life.

Chika Chukwunonso Okpala considered himself lucky to be alive at 73 and be a witness to this book, documenting his life and times on earth! His surviving very close shaves with death informed his sense of gratitude for hitting 70 plus and being counted among the billions of people alive in the land of the living.

In a mirthful attestation, the great TV masquerade in his Zebrudayic exuberance stated; "I, Chief His Royal Palm Wine Powerless, Chief Zebradaya Okrigwe Nwogbo Alias 4.30 would have dead die long time Imo River (long time ago).

But my Chineke God was say no not yet .... that are why I am still here talking with you and still doing things to the jollity of Igwe madu. Are you see what I am saw? Ka Chineke mezie okwu".

The first and the beginning of the spells of his bad and ugly times came way back in the year 2005. This was by a ghastly motor accident that occurred on his way to keep a master of ceremony date at Owerri via Arondizuogu.

On that fateful day, he and his driver had travelled from Enugu to Nnobi, to go to Owerri the next morning from Nnobi. Before they got to Nnobi, they had to stop over to honour an invitation for a birthday party at Awka, which lasted till very late into the night that day. So, in the morning, when they took off for Owerri, he was still feeling very sleepy and asked his driver to drive gradually to enable him to take a nap at the back seat of the car, a Mercedes 230 flat boot.

He recalled they had gone as far as Arondizuogu when his driver collided with another car while trying to overtake a trailer. The impact was such that he was thrown from the back seat to the front with his head banging against the dashboard and his eyeballs pulled out of their socket. In his words;

My driver who miraculously didn't sustain serious injuries, on seeing my state started wailing that he has killed his master. Truly, the situation was ugly.

Even as I was feebly calling him to stop wailing that I was not dead, he did not hear me. Our vehicles were damaged almost beyond repairs. The passersby, who came to our rescue, flagged down another vehicle appealing to the Good Samaritan to rush me to the Okigwe General hospital.

Unfortunately, for him and the driver, when they got there, the hospital was not functioning. He was then taken to a nearby one which was a mushroom hospital by all standards. The doctor was not even on seat and blood was still gushing out. After nearly three hours of waiting, the doctor came back and promptly examined him.

There was no anesthetics to administer, meaning that Chika had to endure the pains as the doctor crudely sutured his popping-out eyeballs. When he was done with his crude and dangerous operation, the doctor declared that the eyes were fine and they should just pay and go. Chika recounted;

Unfortunately, this was not true! Eye specialists

I visited later at Enugu discovered the doctor made

a mistake in his stitching, resulting in my eyes tilting a bit out of balance in its socket. Regrettably, I was told there was nothing more they could do to correct it. I continued to apply GV until it healed up

The aftermath of some hidden effects of the auto crash came some twelve years after, in 2017. This manifested in one of the worse spell of his bad seasons in life. But lucky him, it happened where providence provided rescue for him. He was on invitation performance tour of some states in the USA and had performed successfully in two states. It was when he arrived in Texas, the third state, that tragedy struck. "I started feeling very cold and found out I could not stand, so I asked my promoter to get me a walking stick . . ." Chief Okpala began, sadness all over his voice as he told the pathetic story of what happened to him on his day of performance at Texas.

I managed to get to the venue, but I could not come down from the car. Not seeing me on stage as expected, the huge fans who were so gathered felt I was scamming them. My promoters asked some of them to come and see me in the car, that I had suddenly fallen ill. In desperation, I forced myself out of the car but could not stand. I went down and passed out. I was taken back into the car and rushed to Aman Memorial Hospital, Texas. When I regained consciousness and asked where I was, the doctor told me I've been unconscious for three nights and asked me if I had an accident before? I said yes and told him how it happened.

The doctor then told me that the x-ray they carried out on me revealed that two columns of my spine were decaying and about disjointing. That would have been the end for me if not for God's Grace that made it happen there and not at home in Nigeria.

Going forward, Chief Okpala revealed that the doctors carried out a major surgery on him replacing the decayed columns of his spine with plastics since they could not lay hands on human bones. He was in the hospital for two months and was visited by many of the fans who had come to watch his show especially, fellow Anambrarians in the US. One of his old time friends, Peter Izuako particularly stayed with him and ensured that everything went well in the hospital for those two months he was there. Lucky him again, the huge hospital bills were paid for him by an NGO that preferred not to be mentioned.

This ar surprise me proproly!" the Chief Zebrudaya in him retorted. "When I am ask dem "How much are the charge? They was say no charge. That was surprise surprise!

You mean no charge at all at all? For two months with the chop chop ndeh! Mr. Peter Izuakor was told me .... if they are told me the charge I may faint. But an NGO has paid the charge and are does not want me to thank them. The NGO are philanthropy. I was ask Peter I am hear you proproly? They was laugh at me and said if they are told me the charge I will faint.

And I shouted my 'Jehovah Ammagadam!' Am I hear you proproly? That it ar cost you nothing nde? They laughed and said, You may not be able to pay the money fi you are told'. 'Ok! So who are de people that are pay the money, so I can thank dem proproly? I insisted. They said an NGO that pleaded to offset the bills anonymously. So after much pressure, they said the total cost of my treatment was Eight hundred and fifty thousand dollars. Truly, I couldn't have afforded such huge amount of money. Although, the pains have not completely disappeared, but I remain eternally grateful to the magnanimous NGO that took care of the bills, Peter Izuako and my fellow Anambrarians and indeed, all my fans and people of goodwill in America who came to my rescue. You see! I would have been a goner at 67 in that 2017 when this thing happened. But by his Grace, here I am alive in the land of the living counting plus three extra years upon the bible's 70." Chika rejoiced.

One other sad season that touched him badly was the sudden loss of his first daughter, Adaora at age 16. This was the one who had shown inclinations to toe his footpaths in the industry. Ada was already writing films, helping and guiding her schoolmates to perform drama. His two surviving children have shown no interest at all in the industry.

On the positive note, he had his remarkable times and blissful seasons in his life and career. Apart from his hitting global fame for his humongous success in his career, Chief Okpala considered when they had the first sponsorship from Co-operative and Commerce Bank Ltd (CCB) for the New Masquerade as one of the blissful moments in his career. "It was a big achievement." He attested.

For these blissful moments in the run of his career as an entrepreneur, was equally one very regrettable low moment. This was when they lost sponsorship with Universal Trust Bank (UTB), due to a technical fault.

Gleefully, he recounts that;

For about a decade, the Federal Government of Nigeria always involved the New Masquerade Troupe in National Celebrations. The audience will always watch-out for the New Masquerade Troupe performance as we will be slated to perform last as the climax of entertainment in the celebrations.

Then also came several show performances in Europe and America, powered by Nigerians in Diaspora. In America, we had performed about twelve times in different States of the USA. In England, we had also performed up to ten times.

Down here in Africa, the New Masquerade was always engaged to perform in the Cameroons, Sierra Leone, Liberia and the Gambia.

These fetched him great honours home and abroad as a deserving crown of his great endeavours in his journey through life. This ultimately has seen him evolve as a prophet with honour both at home and abroad.

PART FIVE

CHIKA IN THE EYE OF THE PEOPLE

5.1 A Prophet with Honour at Home and Abroad
5.2 His Men and Mentors
5.3 In the Eye of Close Aides
5. 4 In the Eye of Friends & Felow Actors

It was stated earlier in this book that Chief Chika Okpala – Chief Zebrudaya Okoroigwe Nwogbo; alias 4.30 - is like the proverbial elephant, everyone describes him from the angle he feels him. At this point, we look at public appraisal and testament on his character and personality, through a harvest of candid impressions of what manner of man CHIKA OKPALA is in the eyes of the people. We present some of these views as excerpts of interviews and phone interactions in the following order;

Surviving casts and crew of the New Masquerade

Old Music artistes

Fellow actors and stars of the Nollywood

Finally, the honour and recognition at home and abroad, as well as the mentors through whose paths he walked to fame.

5.1 A PROPHET WITH HONOUR AT HOME AND ABROAD

A prophet is not without honour except in his own hometown and in his own household", says the Holy Book. However, Chika Okpala has proven to be an exception by his strides and impact. He is indeed, a cherished worthy son that has brought great honour to his hometown, Nnobi, his home state, Anambra, Igbo race and his fatherland, Nigeria, with his works. Testifying to this assertion, his kinsman and fellow thespian, Leo Spider Osuji stated; "His (Chika) popularity is as great at home (Nnobi) as it is in the state, across the country and beyond. I give you a little testimonial to this; there was this event that was holding in town in which the state's greats were gathered. At the middle of the event, when the Governor was delivering his speech, Chika sneaked in and took a sit behind. Unknown to him, the master of ceremony had seen him and acknowledged his arrival into the hall. The Governor's then, Willy Obiano paused in his speech and said; "you mean Chief Zebrudaya is in this hall? Let me see him!" he insisted. Chika rose to a thunderous ovation following the Governors accolades and reverence. Such reverences follow him everywhere he goes at home and elsewhere.

Osuji, the Udude Nnobi went on; "Let me also reveal to you here that, what you people see of Zebrudaya today, we had seen in his father, Chief Daniel Okpala who was also a comedian in his own capacity. Even his late elder brother, Chike, was another good comedian known in Nnobi, just that none of them went as far as Chika has gone. . ."

"Beyond Chika's global popularity that has endeared him to the people of all nations who have seen his acts here; Chika Okpala is quite a home boy, a household name in Nnobi. He mixes with people very freely irrespective of their ages. Just like what the father did when he was alive, he mixed with people; played with people, joked with people, so it is with Zebrudaya in Nnobi. You know in life, no human being would go without an enemy, but in Nnobi, I believe that 99.999% of the people love that man, Zebrudaya." Osuji further attested.

In Igbo land generally, one salient index of measuring a man's relevance in his hometown is his relationship with his age grade and role in his community, and their welfare Unions/Associations. Many big men have failed woefully here, forgetting that no matter their height of glory and status in life, when they die, their remains are returned to be buried among the very people they disdained.

Even as a global figure, Chika Okpala not only relates very well with his people, at home, Nnobi and elsewhere, he serves them even at the home union level. As a matter of fact, in the year of writing of this book, Chika was serving as the current Chairman of Nnobi Town Welfare Organization in Enugu.

Before now, I used to represent Nnobi Welfare Organization (NWO) Enugu Branch at General monthly meetings at Nnobi. Thereafter, I was elected Vice Chairman of NOW, Enugu Branch and presently the elected Chairman of Nnobi Welfare Organization Nnobi (NWO), Enugu Branch and by extension a council member of Igwe-in-council, Nnobi.

Chika has essentially lived an exemplary life as a symbol of honour and pride of his people and a role model whose actions and works have influenced many, including Chief Leo Spider Osuji, (Udude Nnobi), a Nollywood star and music artiste of the hit song; Obodo Emebiwo.

Chika single handedly provided and installed electric poles and cables for a street of one kilometre distance named after him in Nnobi.

Again, as a member of the Abalukwu Social Club of Nigeria, Nnobi, he contributed his quota in the club's General Hospital building project for Nnobi. This is as he was equally a contributor towards the procurement of electric transformer for UdideAmadunu village, Nnobi.

In Igbo land, and indeed, most places in Nigeria, the worth and relevance of a man's impact in service to his society/home land is evaluated through worthy recognitions from the society/ hometown. Awards of honour, certificates of recognition, chieftaincy titles etc. constitute the main rudiments of these recognitions.

And verily verily, Chika Okpala has all these in quantum. His collection of awards of honour, certificates of recognition and chieftaincy titles are legendary. With a harvest of over one hundred and fifty of these awards and many more to come, one can say with all modesty, Chief Chika Okpala remains one of the most decorated comic actors and TV personalities alive today in Africa. Chief Chika Okpala - Chief Zebrudaya Okoroigwe Nwogbo alias 4.30 is a holder of two of such national honours; Member of the Order of the Niger (MON) and Member of the Federal Republic (MFR). The MFR honours came in the reign of General Abdulsalmi Abubakar, who ruled the nation [1998 -1999] at the sudden death of General Sani Abacha. Then the MON honours came in the first tenure [1999-2003] of General Olusegun Obasanjo. On the Global front, Chika has the rare honour of being conferred the prestigious United Nations Rescue Noble Ambassador for Peace in Africa.

Just for the records, this haul of national and international honours cuts across professional circles and social/cultural boundaries. On the socio-cultural front, Chief Okpala is a holder of three chieftaincy titles from three states in Igbo land. The titles are, first from his hometown, Nnobi, Anambra State. The second is from Mbaise, Imo State, and the third one from Aba, Abia State. Chieftaincy titles in Igbo land, especially in the past when holders were chosen based on merit, are crowns of glory conferred on worthy sons and daughters in whom the kings and the traditional ruling councils of these communities find worthy and well pleased with their accomplishments and service to the people.

As a media and theatre arts practitioner, Chika's footprints are manifest in broadcasting, advertising, public relations, and management. In the world of advertising, for instance, Chika reveals that he has developed and produced over 500 advert spots/ commercials on television and over 700 advert/commercials on radio, via his Zodiak Brains Films Company.

In the theatre world, promotion of African culture and heritage is his dreams with his Zodiak Brains. Chika stated

> *Some of our trending productions such as; Ejiri mara Igbo, Ahuike di mkpa, Chairman and Son, Mmekpa Ahu", Silent Cries etc. testify to this . . . And we stick to this view... by turning out writers of comedy stuff, Artistes' and Artiste managers as change agents for sustainable socio-economic development with film clips, skits and movies of African setting."*

Given this enviable list of multi-dimensional services/ operations, cutting across professional circles and social boundaries, Chika meritoriously belongs to the following professional bodies:

1. ARCON (formaly APCON) - Advertising Regulatory Council of Nigeria
2. ITPAN - Independent Television Producer Association of Nigeria
3. NIPR - Nigeria Institute of Public Relations
4. NANTAP - National Association of Nigerian Theatre Arts Practitioners
5. NIM - Nigeria Institute of Management

On the social front, Chief Okpala is a reputable member of the Elite Social Club of Nigeria, Aba and served the Club as its Vice President (1975-1978) when Aba was still in Imo state. In 1977, Chika played a leading role in galvanizing youngsters at Aba into forming a philanthropic organization named, Jaycees' Club. This club wrought good works of philanthropy, making regular visits to Cheshire Homes and Orphanages to fete the sick and the poor with gifts contributed in cash and kind by members. He is today one of the living legends of Nollywood and leader of the Nollywood Elders Forum in Enugu.

5.2 HIS MEN AND MENTORS

Ndi Igbo would say; "Ofu osisi anaghi eme ohia belu so enunuebe!" meaning, "A tree does not constitute a forest except for the great Enunuebe (umu nnunu ebe). By nature, man is surely a gregarious being and survives on the existence of others. No one, no matter how great or small he may be, is where he or she may be in life all by himself. Indeed, at any point in life, "we all need somebody to lean on.", say songwriters, Bill Withers and Michael Bolton.

For Chika Chukwukwunonso Okpala, there were quite a number of individuals upon whose shoulders he leaned on to rise to fame. From what we have read so far, his childhood friend and fellow drama enthusiast, late Ogonna Agu ranks the first and earliest in his life. With their Two City Play House, the formation of which was suggested by Ogonna Agu, they teamed up to contribute their own quota to the war efforts for survival of the embattled generation of Igbos of the Civil War era (1967-70).

After the war, when Chika joined others to come to Enugu to hustle for survival, Ogonna providentially surfaced at the most crucial moment at the Red Cross Centre, Enugu to rescue Chika from the dilemma of where to live in Enugu. Ogonna not only accommodated Chika, but also introduced him to the Hill Top Arts Theatre that became Chika's stepping stone to professional acting and broadcasting. It was from here that Chika met his would-be mentors, especially James Iroha and other movers and shakers of the radio and TV industry then. Unfortunately, Chika revealed that quintessential Ogonna Agu was no more.

He lamented;

Oooh! My dear Ogonna Agu is now of the blessed memory. But interestingly, Ogonna later came to take a wife from my family.

I don't know how it happened, but he told me that he was coming to marry from me! And he did come for my cousin Evelyn.

The wife, Evelyn Agu is now a barrister at law. Evelyn schooled at Alvan Ikoku College of Education, Owerri and used to spend her holidays in my house at Aba then.

JAMES AKWARI IROHA.

The next in the line of men he met on his way up, was his main mentor, friend and producer, James Akwari Iroha. Iroha was a recipient of the national honours - Officer of the Order of the Niger (OON). He was the creator of the legendary drama series, The Masquerade. He was the one who recommended and moved for Chika's employment with NTA, Aba upon the creation of states.

Chief Iroha was from Amokwe, Item, of the old Bende Division now in Abia state. He bagged a diploma certificate in Theater Arts from University College, Ibadan. In his comic reference to how Mr. Iroha cherished this academic prowess from Ibadan. Chika jocularly said;

> *James was always bragging and harassing us with his prestigious Diploma from a higher institution just to provoke us to aspire to improve on our academics. So, when Chief Nnanna Ukegbu gave us a grant to run a remedial programme in his TADEM University at Imerienwe, Owerri, we, (Clarus and I) are clutche at the opportunity 'with the two both of our hands, so that we ar hear word for GringoriAkabogu of Ikot 4 and his Diploma Asambodo from Ibadan"*

Before his diploma, Chief Iroha had his early education in Bukuru, Plateau state. Born October 12, 1942, Iroha was indeed, a multitalented individual, a versatile thespian, who incontrovertibly, remains a revered pioneer of the comic acts in the entertainment industry and broadcasting in Nigeria. He was also a songwriter, singer with a sonorous voice and has a couple of music albums to his credit. It is equally on record that Iroha led the Masquerade troupe to the glorious Festival of Arts and Culture (FESTAC) in Lagos in 1977 and was premier Director of Imo state Council of Arts and Culture, (ISCAC) from 1980 – 1982.

This was before the creation of Imo and Anambra states in 1976. The movement of Mr. James Iroha to Imo State with the drama led to the arrival of the programme on NTA, Aba, where other personalities of the broadcasting and entertainment industry held sway. First, was Mazi Anyaogu Elekwachi Ukonu, who at this point in time was Director of Programmes at NTA, Aba and was subsequently appointed the General Manager of the station in November 1978.

Mazi Ukonu was a foremost entertainer and a man of vision who insisted on tangible materials when he came across one in the course of producing his very popular variety show, Mazi Ukonu's Club on NTA Aba. James Iroha, as a producer, worked under him. Mazi Ukonu had to bend when Mr. Iroha insisted that Chika Okpala was a key character in his programme, the Masquerade and should be employed by NTA Aba in other to sustain the programmes and make him available for rehearsals and productions.

> *Mazi had no choice but to employ me to ensure the existence and continuity of a programme that kept the nation awake and entertained . . . and I gave my unreserved services to NTA, Aba . . . I am very grateful to Mazi Ukonu for giving me the opportunity to develop and showcase my talent to the world.*
>
> *To James Iroha, OON, I remain ever grateful to him to have discovered my God given talent as an entertainer and artiste. Iroha introduced me to Chirf Ugorji Eke (Omefuru onyeodiri) who supported and became very fond of me. May their souls rest in peace. . . Amen! Chika prayed. More about James Iroha (OON) in the Appendix page*

MAZI UKONU

The main player in Chika's league of mentors in broadcasting and the entertainment industry was the great, Mazi Anyaogu Elekwachi Ukonu, Madu Oha 1 of Igbere land. He was the big boss of NTA, Aba when Chika was emerging as the Zebrudaya of the Masquerade. Mazi Ukonu was indeed, everything a big boss in the industry should be. He was perhaps, the most exposed of the legends of the entertainment industry and broadcasting in his time. This is given the enviable records of his odyssey in the prestigious American Hollywood, featuring in many movies as far back as the 1 950s/60s. He bagged a Bachelor of Arts degree in Theatre Arts from University of California in Los Angeles.

Before leaving for the USA to prove his inimitable talent in the arts, he had his primary education at the Central School, Igbere, his hometown between 1936 and 1944. He attended Hope Waddell Training Institute, Calabar, for his secondary education between 1944 and 1949. He was employed in the public service of the Eastern Nigeria Government in January 1950.

Worthy of note here is that Chika Okpala who was born in June that year (1950) was barely two months old when Mazi Ukonu left his public service Job in August and sailed to the USA with the hope of reading medicine.

Instead of bemoaning and getting frustrated at the overwhelming circumstances that changed his intentions of studying medicine in the USA, versatile Ukonu exploited his God-given talent to the fullest to establish himself into a colossus of comedy, movies and variety show presenter/producer in the USA.

A man with intense African pride and predilection to his roots,

Ukonu tilted towards promotion of African values and culture to his American audience and so excelled to the level of co- performing with the Great Caribbean iconic thespian, Harry Belafonte and his troupe at Riviera Hotel in Las Vegas, Nevada.

That was not all, from 1953, while still in the USA, Mazi Ukonu was said to have produced, directed and starred in the Annual African Harvest Festival staged at the University of Southern California in Los Angeles, where African students projected their cultural heritage. Three years into this in 1956, he became the manager, producer and star performer of a monthly stage variety show popularly known as Ukonu African Nite Life in Los Angeles. This is surely the progenitor of the popular Ukonu Club, he replicated in Aba on his return to homeland, Nigeria. Mazi Ukonu with his Afro Calypsonian Band produced three (3) albums

Mazi Ukonu actually returned to Nigeria in 1960 and on July 1, 1960, he joined the Eastern Nigeria Broadcasting Corporation (ENBC) as a Senior Producer. He later rose through various higher positions in the establishment through thick and thin of the civil war years. It was when he became Head of Variety and Light Entertainment programme and later, Controller Programmes, at Aba station in 1974 that he introduced the famous Ukonu's Club. The Programme under his charge, not only fulfilled its entertainment mission on air, but also became a veritable hub for parading and promoting budding and established talents.

Mazi became Director of Programmes at NTA, Aba in April 1976 and a year later in 1977, he was appointed the Acting General Manager of the station. He was confirmed the substantive General Manager in November 1978. He bowed out of service of the NTA in May 1984. Little wonder a tribute in his burial programme summed up his indelible footprints in the industry thus;

"It is hard to overstate the debt we owe great men and women of genius. Mazi returned from overseas and saw that drama in our land was a show of western culture. The whole civilized world believes in the theatre; the society wants the great dramatist; the society is prepared to pay handsomely to anyone who can worthily put our age on the stage. With apologies to modesty, but there is no immodesty in speaking the truth; one of the world's greatest dramatists, who has transformed the darkness of thought and devaluation of culture in Nigerian, is Mazi Ukonu, who by impersonal agency of art, revolutionized thought and attitude and has touched and kindled theatre arts, drama and music to reflect our African culture. Mazi is owed a great debt for his originality and transformational contributions in the field of theatre arts. Chief Zebrudaya Okoroigwe Nwogbo alias 4:30 appeared on stage at Igbere for the funeral ceremony for Mazi Ukonu in 2020. That appearance reignited the 1984 vision of Chief Alexander Nkwere Iheke for the publication of this book which was originally conceived as "Zeburudaya in Pictures" when Mazi Ukonu was General Manager of NTA Aba.

And this iconic Mazi had three great music albums he produced in the USA along with his kinsman Dr. John Obidiah Iboko, the drummer to leave a footprint of his peregrination of the music industry in his thespian life.

PAUL AKALONU

Grateful that Chika did not forget the Controller Programmes he worked under then at NTA, Aba, Ndaa Paul Akalonu aka The big Boy. Quite old and still kicking at the time of writing, Akalonu remains one of Nigeria's greatest music producers and talent promoters of our time. Many superstars and groups of the music artistes, in the 1980s and early 1990s, passed through him. Christy

Essien Igbokwe was mentored and produced by Paul Akalonu as she was a recurring guest at the famous Mazi Ukonu's Club. Akalonu was the producer of super-pop groups including the Apostles, led by Walton Arungwa, The Sweet Breeze etc. Reflecting on Chika, the old big boy said; "Chika is a good boy and a born super star comedian and entertainer, a worthy subordinate in whom he (Akalonu) and all who mentored him (Chika) as a young producer in NTA, Aba then were all well pleased"

PETER IGHO

While Mazi Ukonu was holding sway in NTA, Aba in the East, a younger warrior of the tube, Peter Igho was holding sway in Jos and later, Lagos, the then headquarters of the National Television, as one of the most creative and prolific programme producer to pass through the NTA. Though born and brought up in Jos, hence, often mistaken to be from the Middle Belt, Igho is actually of Delta State origin. He is a multi-linguist, teacher and quintessential content creator on TV.

From this book, it is obvious that Igho was one of the men whose creativity brought to life the golden era of NTA and indeed the TV industry in the 1980s and 1990s in Nigeria. Apart from producing the highly entertaining and memorable drama series, Cock Crow at Dawn, Igho gave national life to the diverse culture of the pluralistic nationalities of Nigeria via the National TV. He recharged the regional sitcoms and appropriated it for the NTA Network Programme's Service. Creatively, he attached the prefix "New" to the titles of these regional star programmes to indicate its new status as a national programme without them losing their root, originality and established aura and audience loyalty over the years in their various regions. Some of these series were; The Village Headmaster, which became The New Village Headmaster from the Western Zone, The Masquerade as The New Masquerade from the East, The Cock Crow at Dawn – New Cock Crow at Dawn from the North Central Zone, The New Samanja to reflect life of the military men in the barracks. He mentored and annexed the regional producers into the network fold without dislocating them from the services of their zonal home base. What a new Sultan of Programmes at the Network Service of the NTA! Interestingly, Chief Chika Okpala, the great Zebrudaya Okoroigwe Nwogbo alias 4.30 is one of those regional producers he mentored, annexed and built from regional to national stars. What does Peter Igho say of Chika Okpala?

"Over the years, millions of Nigerians who have watched content on their TV screens will acknowledge that Chief Chika Okpala, Zebrudaya in the evergreen drama series Masquerade, is easily one of the best actors Nigeria has been blessed with. His brilliant use of his unique language, his spontaneous response in any situation and the numerous awards that he has garnered through many years of bringing joy and laughter through satire, mark him out as a true legend. However, Chika Okpala is much more than an actor. He worked closely with me when I was producing the iconic series Cock Crow at Dawn. He added great value to the production, always punctual at call times and showing great dedication to whatever assignment he is given. It is no wonder that when he was assigned the production of Masquerade he excelled and successfully handled the series for many years.

He is fully committed to his work and never allows personal problems affect or deter him. I recall when his daughter was in hospital. He would leave her ward and head back to the studios to record. He exemplifies the great Nigerian entertainers who put their hearts and souls into their jobs at the expense of their families and loved ones. The show must go on!

This is especially important for Chika who is a loving family man. He is also very respectful, never allowing his success to affect his relationships, young and old, friends and colleagues"

In every generation in history, there appears a character very special and unique who stands out and is irreplaceable. Chief Chika Okpala, Zebrudaya Okorigwe Nwogbo Alias 4.30 is one such Nigerian. I am happy and honoured to know him and to have worked closely with him"

5.3: IN THE EYE OF SURVIVING CASTS & CREW CHIEF (MRS.) LIZZY EVOEME - OVULARIA

I was popularly known as Misisim Ovularia Urediya Nwogbo alias G4, but my real name is Chief (Mrs.) Lizzy Evueme. I was born (January, 1942) in Calabar of Cross River State today. I am a native of Akabo in Ikeduru Local Government of Imo State. I was married to Mr. Israel Erondu Evueme of Umuaba village in Obioma Ngwa, Osisioma Local Government of Abia state.

How I joined the Masquerade drama series

I had always loved acting right from childhood. And since it was my childhood love, when I eventually stumbled into it, it was a dream fulfilled. I had long married, had my children and sadly, had also lost my husband before I was discovered via joining the New Masquerade. However, I had been acting before the Masquerade group came from Enugu into Aba at the creation of Imo State. There was a show, Sons and Daughters, James Iroha was producing and they were looking for somebody to play a short role, and one of my colleagues in the other team we had then mentioned me to James. I was called for an audition; I passed and was chosen to act that part. After that, I was a regular observer in the masquerade drama until the lady who was acting the chief's wife at that time left for the US and they needed someone to take her place. So, James asked me if I could do it, I told him to try me. After the test, he declared me passed. That was how I got into the show.

My role and relationship with Zebrudaya

The Ovularia I played was a housewife and a mother. A good mother is always an adviser, a stabilizer and a shock absorber all rolled into one to her husband and children. In my real life I was a bit of all those. So I simply brought all three together into the role of Ovularia and Chief Zebrudaya as husband was not an easy person to go along with. Nevertheless, amongst all in the cast, Chika Okpala – my Zeby oo . . as I call him, was my best friend on the set and he was quite unsparing whenever I or anyone at all go astray and he will harshly, very harshly correct me. So, also did I do to him whenever he goofs too as human being he is. We were indeed one happy family, both on and off stage, but sometimes, we had our misunderstandings and disagreements. And for a role model, Sisi Clara of the Village Headmaster inspired me a lot. She was my role model in the Industry.

The language of the drama

James Iroha was producing and mostly, he was writing the script. It was him who coined the language that they started with when we were acting locally based in NTA, Aba. But later on when we went national, a lot of other writers joined the team of writers and were bringing scripts. As for the language, it was chiefly James Iroha who coined the language. Though, sometimes we also made our own inputs. And since the public accepted it, they loved it, they liked it, they accepted it, we went along with it.

Popularity and criticism of the Masquerade

There's a proverb in Ngwa dialect that says; "Oha abughi uto", "Oha abughiiro"; meaning, not everybody will like you and not everybody will hate you or what you are doing. The critics we got were essentially from few individuals, not that kind of popular protest from everybody. The New Masquerade was no doubt very popular with the people and they were hailing it saying; "Oh! That programme, that programme!" But I know not everybody liked us. Some didn't like the language. For instance, when Jegede was there, and was speaking his Yoruba, a lot Yoruba people didn't like him. They said he was bastardizing the language. When Zebrudaya speaks his English, a lot of English Nigerians or Nigerian English men said he was killing the English language. Some people saw Ovularia as a peacock. So it was individualistic, according to Oyibo grammarians. Indeed, it was a case of, you like some, and you don't like some.

REV. DAVIS OFFOR – CLARUS MGEOJIKWE

I am Rev Davis Offor, at the moment, a priest in the Aetherius Spiritual Brotherhood worldwide. I have been a comedian right from my childhood, comedy is in my blood. I inherited it from my parents. Now, I am in my 80s with this sight impairment, I believe God will heal me someday. I have no other choice than to retire to my priestly duties and that's where I am now here at Aba. But you cannot take away comedy completely from me. That's what I have enjoyed right from my childhood.

Corroborating the origin of the Masquerade drama

The famous Masquerade drama series of the NTA started in Enugu after the war as a radio programme. The title then was "In a Lighter Mood". On radio, the character, Zebrudaya was known as Chief Josephat Okoroigwe Nwaogbo. James Iroha was the principal producer and I was a junior producer under him. It was when the drama advanced to the TV that the Chief character's name changed to Zebrudaya, with all the adjustments.

Zebrudaya had other wives; the first was Celina Ugodiya Nwaogbo who featured while we were at Enugu. Celina dropped when we moved to NTA Channel 6, Aba at the creation of Anambra and Imo states in 1976. Kate Chima took over as the next wife of Chief Zebrudaya with the name Getrude Appolonia Godgive Nwogbo of Umudele, in Ukwa divide. It was when Kate left us for the USA that Lizzy Evueme came in as Ovularia, the last and longest serving wife of Chief Zebrudaya.

When the drama was taken over as NTA Network programme with our boss, Peter Igho as Executive Producer, we were relocated back to Enugu, the NTA Zonal Headquarters. And the name changed to The New Masquerade.

Relationship with Chika and other crew members

We related very well with ourselves on and off the set. Chika who was our youngest was Chief Zebrudaya Okoroigwe Nwaogbo alias 4.30, the major character and he got our respect as his houseboys. And I, Clarius, have way of making the government know the feelings of the masses. There were certain things we may feel that was not going well with the government and then, we just try to pinch their buttocks and they would sit up in realization of what they should do. Truly, the public loved the programme and when it went into the NTA network, the entire country enjoyed the programme at that time and the government recognized what we were doing through the network.

The unique language of the cast

James Iroha, who was the producer of the programme and scriptwriter, coined the language. Somehow, many other writers had equally emerged for the programme including, Chika and myself. The scripts had to follow the language pattern originated and established for each character by the producer, James Iroha. So, individual characters had their own language pattern as was seen in the drama. By dint of many rehearsals and practice, proficiency sets in and the language pattern becomes part of the role player. Chika fitted into his role so well that it has become his second nature.

On the side effects of the language

Well, there were two sides of it; people up till today still recall the language and some even try to speak it better than Zebrudaya or any of us. The other side, some people believe the language was sort of corrupting school children, who instead of speaking good English, may go with Zebrudaya's English. The point here is that there are tendencies of school children trying to imitate and communicate in that manner of speaking in English which is surely unhealthy for their development.

Choosing comedy format

Comedy as a format of drama presents an air of peace and exhilaration not an attack or confrontation. It is one safe medium for satire in drama. So, while entertaining the audience, serious messages that drew attention to crucial public issues were embedded and jocularly passed. This is what we were doing with the New Masquerade then. It became a widely accepted satirical drama piece used to pinch the buttocks of the government. In most cases, they reacted favorably to the messages passed through what they were watching in those scenes. The public loved the way we presented programme as it gave them that sense of relaxation after all the hullabaloos of the day's work. This is why the Thursday nights the programme was on air were like mini festive nights across the land.

Today, some comedians are now making their millions doing what we were doing just to bring joy and laughter to the people. As you can see, there are some of us who started it that are languishing in hunger land . . . you know, but that's life, somebody has to get the shot from the beginning, then others would afterwards follow and reap the gains and glory.

CLAUDE EKE – PRINCE JEGEDE

I, Honourable PRINCE, DR. JEGEDE SHOKOYA, son of the soil, and the great grandson of the Idi of Idi Araba and by the grace of God, the only young millionaire in the whole universe . . . tori Olonwu! This was the typical self-conceiting introduction many of us watching the New Masquerade heard from this Yoruba Character named Jegede Shokoya. Little did we know that this was a typical

Okoro Igbo! In short from Mbaise in Imo State and his real name was CLAUDE EKE! Indeed, Eke was gorgeous to watch displaying his peacock mannerism of a true Yoruba Prince in his flowing Agbada and fold cap to match.

He was indeed, the most loquacious and gregarious in the pack of the superlative talents that made the new Masquerade the most endearing of all sitcoms to hit the nation from the Eastern Coast of Nigeria. He depicted to the full the typical idiosyncrasies of ebullient and elitist men of the west in Nigeria. He was matchless in his role and was quite consistent and loyal to the Masquerade project till death did him part with the show and fellow thespians on November 11, 2002.

CHRISTY ESSIEN IGBOKWE (MFR) [1960-2011]
AKPENOR

Christy Uduak Essien Igbokwe, (MEMBER OF THE FEDERAL REPUBLIC) ranked the most versatile and multilingual female songstress Nigeria ever had in her life time. She sang Ibibio/Efik, her native dialect, Igbo, Yoruba, Hausa, and English languages. She was a native of Okat, Onna, now in Akwa Ibom state. She lost her mother early and was brought to live with a good friend of her mother at Aba. It was this woman (name not given) that discovered Christy's singing proclivity and encouraged her.

This great foster mother was said to have bought her a fairly used cassette tape recorder to be recording her songs. It seems Christy paid more attention to Music than Acting. Nevertheless, she cut her teeth in acting with the New Masquerade on television. She played the role of Akpenor, the cantankerous wife of the egoistic Yoruba man who paraded his regal background as the honourable Dr. Prince Jegede Shokoya, the grandson of Idi of Idiaraba.

Her inimitable performance of this role in the New Masquerade launched her into national fame before her music. Christy was said to have landed herself the role of Akpenor after she was said to have assisted a cast get his role right during one of their rehearsals of the drama show for recording. Ndaa Paul Akalonu was part of her music success as a producer.

Christy rose to be the first female president of the Performing Musicians Association of Nigeria (PMAN) in 1996. Christy married Edwin Igbokwe when she was barely 19 years. She remained a faithful wife and responsible super star mother to her four sons and family till 30th June 2011, when she passed on in Lagos before her 51st birthday.

ROMANUS AMUTA – NATTY (1943 – 2022)

Born 1943, ROMANUS AMUTA who played the role Natty Okosisi was one of those pioneer casts of the Masquerade before it mutated to the New Masquerade. Amuta was from

Ukana in Udi LGA of Enugu state. He joined the crew at Aba to complete the circle of pioneer Casts of the Masquerade to drive and sustain the sitcom at NTA, Aba in 1977. His lanky and hungry visage, his unique way of using his body language to communicate comically, his unstrained gluttony at the sight of food, made Romanus an apt Cast and matchless in his role.

He never said no to invitation to join the table or has such time to wait to be invited. He had a knack at arriving at auspicious moments when food is served in Zeby's house and will make straight to the table without washing his hands. In occasions madam Ovularia insists he should go wash his hands before joining, Natty will comically roll up his sleeves and even his trousers, wash his hands to his elbows, adjusting and salivating visibly in sheer rapaciousness. He was so good at his role that his name - Naatty and his alias Commissioner-for-longer-throat' became synonymous with greediness with children in real life.

Romanus sustained his role without replacement all through the dynamic mutations of the New Masquerade as a result of the exit of many of the pioneer actors and entrance of new Casts assigned new roles and names to keep the Masquerade family and world going. He battled with real hardship and ailments and passed on February 10, 2022, at age 79 in a Lagos hospital.

VERONICA NJOKU – RAMOTA

Vero Njoku was one of those ex staff of NTA who chose to resign and join the Independent production world. She was the replacement of Christy Essien Igbokwe – Akpenor as wife of the loquacious Jegede Shokoya in the new Masquerade family. Vero was equally multi lingual and very good in the role. Not many new she was Igbo and not Yoruba. She was even more cantankerous than Akpenor and matched Jegede fire for fire. She was by all means a Dame of the movie Industry. Painfully, too Vero had also passed on 22 March, 2017.

TONY AKPOSHERI – (ZACHY)

Tony sees Chief Chika Okpala as a close confidant, mentor and Father.

"I am Chief's boy, he's been a big mentor and father to me and that is the way he takes me. One thing I like him a lot for is that he's someone who likes teaching. He doesn't hoard knowledge; he believes in sharing what he knows about something. This is like Peter Igho, our mutual boss in NTA, Lagos. Chika took after him in that and I took after Chika. He is a great man and a team player. When I wedded my wife from Nkanu land, he and all the Masquerade crew were there for me."

Tony added that Chief Chika Okpala was a stickler for rules and agreements. "One other thing I like about him too is that Chief is a man who honours agreement. If for instance you agree to do a job with him for one Naira, Chief will pay you one Naira in the end . . . if the agreement is that you will get one million in the job, Chief will pay you your one million, whether he's gaining or losing . . . Chief Zebrudaya for you. He has touched lives and mentored many, of which I am a testimony . . . Of course, as an actor and producer, he's very good in this job and we see him as a standard bearer especially in the world of comedy."

DR. FRANK JACKSON OGBONNAYA – CLOSE AIDE/COLLEAGUE

Dr. Ogbonnaya is more of Chief Chika Okpala's family member than a close associate, friend and colleague. He lived with him for over 20 years in Enugu serving as his production manager and technical head of his advertising company, Zodiak Brains Films Ltd. A native of Arochukwu, and also a former staff (Cameraman) at NTA Channel 6, Aba, Dr. Ogbonna was one of those who resigned to toe the line of independent production.

"Chika Okpala, (Chief Zebrudaya) is quite a humble and simple man, an intelligent and creative God-fearing individual. In his own small way, he qualifies to be called a philanthropist for he believes in touching the lives of people and encouraging the education of people around him. He never prevaricates in lending support in whichever way he could to build up hard working people like him. A result-oriented person, Chief is always ready to keep sleepless nights to achieve a good production. This is part of what gave the New Masquerade project its huge success under his watch and management. He is a widely travelled man, home and abroad; and rides the crest of public goodwill everywhere he goes for his great role as Chief Zebrudaya in the New Masquerade"

5.4 IN THE EYE OF FRIENDS & FELLOW ACTORS

PETE EDOCHIE (MON) – FELLOW ACTOR AND NOLLYWOOD GREAT

Chief Pete Edochie, Member of the Order of the Niger (MON), as an actor and broadcaster, is a household name in Nigeria, Africa and beyond. He hails from Nteje in Oyi LG of Anambra state. Born March 7, 1947, Chief Edochie reflectively stated; "I am 76 years old this year (2023). I was born at Makurdi, because my father worked with the Nigeria Railways there".

Chief Edochie had his early education in Zaria (1952-59) and St. John's College, Kaduna (1959-64). He joined his father in the services of the railways in 1965 while running a course in journalism and television. This enabled him to join the Eastern

Nigeria Broadcasting Corporation (ENBC) in 1967 on passing the interview.

With the three years run of the ugly war in the land, Chief Edochie thus experienced war journalism as a rookie broadcaster. At a stage, he rose to become the pioneer director of the ABS 3 FM Stereo, and the Director of programmes in the Anambra Broadcasting Service (ABS) when states were created in 1976. He retired from the service of the state broadcasting service in the 1980s. As already stated he played the lead role in the English version of Things Fall Apart in 1985 shortly after he retired from Anambra Broadcasting Service.

"And by that time, Nollywood was still slumbering in the womb of time; it was about seven years after we did Things Fall Apart that Nollywood swung into operation with Living in Bondage.

Well, I retired, Nollywood embraced me and I haven't regretted it ever since and I thank the Almighty God too that my faculties are still intact because for many people my age

dementia has already set in and it is no longer easy for them to recollect events around them let alone take their lines in the thespian profession. So, I thank God", Edochie prayed

On meeting Chika Okpala

Q: Sir, when and how did you meet your fellow superstar actor and broadcaster, Chief Chika Okpala – the Chief Zebrudaya Okoroigwe Nwogbo alias 4.30.?

PETE: Nhnn! Chika met us we didn't meet him, because he was a younger version of those in the industry who were toiling then. I was a staff of the then ENBC. Chika was not a staff. As a matter of fact, Bob Nwangoro, Peter Edochie, Nwora Asika, James Iroha, all of us got together to create the Masquerade. And when we created the Masquerade, the very first Chief Zebrudaya was Nwora Asika. Nwora did a couple of episodes. On the day he (Nwora) did not come, there was a very young man who volunteered to try, and that young man was Chika Okpala. Chika was so young that we required making him up. And for him to look the part, we gave him the tommy. Chika proved a very creative young man. He converted his limitations into an asset. That's why I must always congratulate him.

I must candidly add that, by the time Chika took over that production, his English was not very good, and like I said he converted that to an asset. I remember the first time he wanted to pronounce "Chief" he said "Chieef." We felt as though he was being whimsical. After some time it became clear that there was no need for Nwora Asika to go back to that programme. Chika had given that role an identity that nobody could challenge and he became an instant celebrity, a very big superstar. James Iroha as the producer was there and the other one, Davis Offor and other members of the cast that made the programme one of the most successful programmes ever created on that station and credit must be given to Chika Okpala and James Iroha the producer.

On his relationship/assessment

Q: As superstar actors what is your relationship like?

PETE: Oh well, we have been friends and it's still on. Although we don't see all the time, but whenever we meet, we try to relive our good old times. One other thing I know of him is that Chika is not a free spender. For instance, when people see celebrities and sing in front of them they are expected to part with something to appreciate the singers, Chika is not good at that, I must tell you. . . he's a humour merchant (Laughter).

Q: You have assessed Chika quite positively; let's look at him and the Nollywood. How do you assess his acting generally apart from the comic roles he plays?

PETE: Chika hasn't featured too prominently in Nollywood. He is an immensely successful performer, but he is more of one type actor. Nevertheless, he is one of the Nollywood greats and we Igbos are proud of him, – the famous Zebrudaya Okroigwe Nwogbo, alias 4.30.

LEO-SPIDER OSUJI (UDUDE NNOBI)

Chief Leo Spider Osuji (Udude Nnobi), actor, singer and songwriter, retired senior director of the UNTH, Enugu. He is Chika Okpala's kinsman from Nnobi in Idemili South LG, of Anambra State, Nigeria. He is a member of the Nollywood Elders Forum in Enugu.

Meeting Chika and joining acting

Q: How well do you know Chief Chika Okpala and when did you meet him for the first time?

SPIDER: Yes, I do know him very well. He is a kinsman and from the area of my community called Ifite Nnobi. The first time I met him was way back in 1976, when he was Public Relations Officer of GION Nigeria Ltd. Somebody introduced us saying to him; "Chika, here is your younger brother, they call him Spider Osuji; Spider, here's Zebrudaya, and you've been worrying me to see him". And he made me to come for an audition. And that was about 1989/90, when we started working together and I was still single then.

My brother, this acting thing is not easy oo! I didn't know it has a lot of risks involved then. I don't forget one of those occasions I was brought home around 1 a.m and I wanted to quit. As I alighted from the car in front of my house that night, I said to him; "brother I am not acting again.' He looked at me and laughed mirthfully saying; "my brother Bongos Ikwe ar talk it, 'nothing good comes easy . . .' so you must persevere."

Let me also reveal to you here that, what you people see of Zebrudaya today we had seen in his father Chief Daniel Okpala who was also a comedian in his own capacity. Even his late elder brother, Chike was another good comedian known in Nnobi, just that none of them went as far as Chika has gone.

Q: So, can we then say this is something that runs in the family?

SPIDER: Ooh you can say that again! If I must go further, I can tell you that I have worked with Zebrudaya in some Nollywood productions. As at now, he is the Chairman of the Elders Forum of Nollywood here in Enugu, and most importantly, he is the chairman of our Nnobi Town Welfare Organization, Enugu branch.

His footprints of honour at home

SPIDER: I won't have to start pointing out one after the other, his works or impact on the people because his actions influenced me positively. Even I was motivated by his acting. The question is how do you measure the prowess and values of someone in his society? Is it not by recognition? Chief Chika Okpala is highly recognized by the people and the traditional ruler as a worthy son of Nnobi land for his great endeavour in life.

Rating his performance and character traits

SPIDER: Well, for every man, whatever he is doing, can never be above the limitations of human imperfection. Remember when they reigned, it was difficult to see a good comedian, but all have seen that he proved his mettle. Even up till now what he did in the past is still speaking for him. As an artiste he remains outstanding, and even at this age, he still makes people laugh everywhere he goes. So, for people to accept what he is doing at this age is evidence he knows his onions.

Q: A little flashback please, as somebody you have known and worked closely with, what would you say about his character then and now, I mean, your candid assessment of Chika as a person?

SPIDER: He is someone who doesn't take half measure in what he does. Perfection is his other name when he is doing production. I remember the first time I acted with him and I did something that was not up to his taste he said; "oh Spider that is a very beautiful nonsense you have done there!" That is a man who's ready to influence you if you're ready to learn from him. He may have his own bad sides especially in production. He could be very scathing and chastising, may be because he had over time come to realize that if you're soft, people will leak you like sweet, but if you're bitter like bitter kola, people will not chew you anyhow. So, when he is harsh, as per being real hard on you, you will come to learn in the end he did not mean all he was doing or saying, rather it was just to get the best out of the artiste in you.

Q: Yeah! In terms of morality and sincerity with money, what is he like?

SPIDER: Well, when it comes to things like this, you can't vouch for anyone hundred percent. Many may have said that Chief Zebrudaya cheated them, but for me, all the time we have worked together I didn't experience such negative behavior from him. Instead, I make bold to say he is rather someone who will ensure you get what is due for you in productions. He doesn't owe people.

What I can add here from experiences gathered in the field, some people most times over value themselves and expect more than they deserve, so when at the point of payment, they get what is below their greedy expectation but actually the due for the work they have done, they begin to peddle gossips.

Two, there's this thing called goodwill in accounting; It goes that when you use your goodwill to attract a deal, say hundred-thousand-naira deal, it is expected that you, the one that attracted that deal is entitled to about 40% of that deal. Some artiste will expect Zebrudaya to share out everything equal and when he holds on to what is due to him they will say he is cheating them. I have worked with him and in two or three occasions, what I got from jobs done with him was way more than what I expected from him. Well, there's this man in my place his title name is Onyemetalu Uwa Mma, meaning; who can please the world? No one can please everyone at the same time. Some will talk good while some more will talk bad of you. For me Chief is far above average in this rating.

Q: Finally, sir, what would you remember Chief Chika Okpala for?

SPIDER: I will remember Zebrudaya for two things. One! A man calmed nerves and made people to relax in the midst of high tension. This is through his actions with the old and New Masquerade. Note, he was the youngest in the crew, and was meant to act the role Natti, but because of the way he acquitted himself when he was tried with the lead role he broke history and fame with it. Two! I will remember him as one who influenced a lot of people positively. One remarkable imprint of his that remains eternal of Zebrudaya, (not Chika Okpala) is that unique language of his, understood by all but never known to have been spoken by anyone else . . . Are you are! Are you see what I am saw? It's a language which if one follows will go astray in English language . . . but it sold widely with him as a unique colloquial essentially for entertainment. So, two things, entertainment and jokes and influencing people are the main things I will remember Chika Okpala - Chief Zebrudaya Okoroigwe Nwogbo, alias 4.30 for.

CLEMSON-CORNELL AGBOGIDI – FELLOW ACTOR

Amb. Clemson-Cornell Agbogidi Nnonyelu, ex-civil servant, freelance model, advert agent etc. is one of the popular faces of Nollywood in Nigeria. He is most famous for his Chief priest roles in movies. This has earned him many aliases such as "Agbogidi Nollywood;" "Alusi nwelu ibobo fulu ogu ju nri" – meaning; "the fiery Deity that ignores propitiation for a fight." He is a native of Umuzocha in Awka town, Awka South LGA, Anambra State. As a civil servant, he worked in the registrar's office of the University of Nigeria, Enugu Campus and later as a Personnel Supervisor in IAS Cargo/Courier Services Nigeria Ltd. He had occasionally played minor roles in the popular New Masquerade, Ken Saro Wiwa's Basi & Co comedy series as guest artist in the early 90's. His debut film was Mysteries of Cowries in 1988.

His impression of Chief Okpala

Given the length of time I have known and worked with Chief Chika Okpala aka Chief Zebrudaya [MON, MFR], I simply say; the man is a legendary genius of our time, a no nonsense officiator of events and a man straight as ramrod. My relationship with him as a fellow actor and chairman of Elders Forum of Nollywood Actors, Enugu state chapter is cordial. What I like most about him is his glorious creativity. He carved a niche for himself with his unique language of ZEBRUADYISM. This peculiar language has made him unique and unrivalled in that particular area (Comedy) of the performing art.

Nevertheless, my turn off with him is his inclination to being fixed in his opinion. Nollywood today is characterized by envy and character assassination. Chief Okpala has had more than a fair share of such picketing and this has not in any significant way affected his urbane status and colossal height in the industry.

WALTON ARUNGWA (THE APOSTLES BAND) – HIS OLD TIME FRIEND

Walton Arungwa, the indefatigable songwriter, singer, producer and leader of the defunct Apostles band is alive and kicking albeit old and retired to modest home-based life at his Umunevo Nvosi community of Isiala Ngwa South LGA, Abia State. Arungwa is now a high chief and traditional Prime Minister of his Isiala Nvosi autonomous community. Giving his own impression of Chika Okpala (Chief Zebrudaya), Chief Arungwa, recalled with nostalgia that Chika was a longtime friend in their heydays at Aba. In his words

"Zebrudaya was such a simple person. You will never know he is the Zebrudaya when he walks in the street. He will make you laugh all the time you are with him. In fact, all of them doing the Masquerade drama on TV then at Aba were a great crew and a very happy set of entertainers, although sometimes you will hear them quarreling, over who is in charge . . . Chika – Zebrudaya, James Iroha - Giringori and Davis Offor - Clarius."

PAULSON KALU (ICONIC MUSIC LEGEND) - HIS OLD TIME FRIEND

Chief Paulson Kalu is one of the surviving music superstars in the land. Iconic Kalu from Ohafia Udumeze, in the old Bende LGA of Abia State is in his early 80s. He has retired into a quiet life at Umuahia, the state capital.

In his early day in music, he cut his musical teeth and tutelage with the great Highlife music maestro of his time, late Osita Osadebe. Paulson Kalu, a sensational thriller with his philosophical tunes like Arungwa of his Apostles band, was also occasionally paraded for a regular live band stand show at the Mazi Ukonu's Club variety show at Aba in the 1970s. It was here in this club that Paulson Kalu came in contact with young Chika Okpala, who was then a producer/performer in the Masquerade drama show. Chief Kalu said he struck a friendly relationship with Chika Okpala essentially because he admired and enjoyed his superlative comic acts, just as he admires and enjoys Mr. Ibu (John Okafor) today.

Chief Kalu believes Chika Okpala is incomparable in his act and has made a huge success of his life. In his words; Chika Okpala's all-round success lies in his humane and humble nature, added to his natural inclination to seeking and bringing fun and laughter to all who come across him. Chika is a very likable man from what I have known of him since our days together in Mazi Ukonu's Club live show on NTA Channel 6, Aba.

One day, he visited me at Ohafia, on our way, he saw our people performing the 'uri aha' – the war dance, the way Chika turned and demonstrated the dance made even the players and dancers burst out laughing. Such a natural comic actor, even in his movement and body language, Chika Okpala brings peace and joy everywhere he is. His wife and children must be having fun with him around.

UCHE OGBUAGU AND CHIEF ZEBRUDAYA.

Chief Zebrudaya Okoroigwe Nwaogbo alias 4.30 has enjoyed a father and son relationship with Rt. Hon. Uche Ogbuagu.

It could be recalled that the Imo born Entertainer and Creative Media Principality Uche Ogbuagu has garnered a lot of invaluable experience from the living legend Chief ZB as a foster son and professional ally for decades.

According to Uche,"Chief Zebrudaya is an integral part of me", He has inspired my Media & Entertainment Ministry so immeasurably.

His sense of industry and PR in Showbiz is uncommon.

Even with overwhelming fame and Global acceptance, He is still very humble and unassuming. "Most times, I don't even remember to eat or rest whenever there is a job to be done, is a trait I got from Workaholic Chief ZB" says Uche Ogbuagu.

Uche Ogbuagu has enjoyed an age long robust affinity with Chief Zebrudaya.

Ogbuagu, from his secondary school days, has been around Chief ZB and the New Masquerade family. During School Holidays and Midterm breaks, he usually visits his big auntie, Ovularia at 2nd Avenue, Trans Ekulu Enugu.

The closeness he enjoyed with the Cast and Crew of the New Masquerade TV series back then played very tremendous role, inspiring Ogbuagu to higher heights in Artistry.

Towards the end of his studentship, he was already a stage performer, Stand Up Comedian and label owner. In the year 1999, he released his comedy collabo series "Laughter Junction" where he

Featured Chief ZB, 4.30 Nkem Owoh A.k.a Osuofiason

Sam Loco Efe

James Iroha A.k.a Gringory

Claude Eke A.k.a Jegede Shokoya and a Host of other anointed Entertainers. He has had several live shows with Chief ZB within Nigeria and Overseas including Dubai UAE.

Uche has co- featured and co-produced several Radio and Television Advertisements with Chief ZB for Private and corporate entities, including Governments.

Uche Ogbuagu, before his foray into politics, wherein he became a Special Adviser to Government of Imo State on Entertainment Matters and later a Legislator who represented Ikeduru and subsequently the Majority Leader of the 9th Imo State Legislature has remained very close to Chief Zebrudaya and family, as their bonds are beyond professional ties.

Ogbuagu's Auntie- Late Chief Mrs. Lizzy Evoeme(Ovuleria) who hails from Akabo Ikeduru, same as Uche Ogbuagu was the on screen wife to Chief Zebrudaya.

These icons, have continued to show mastery as well as play role models to many upcoming artistes and Creative Media Minds who desire to grow through their tutelage unto excellence.

OLIVER O. MBAMARA – FRIEND AND FELLOW ACTOR

With humility, I write to express my gratitude for the opportunity to contribute even a paragraph on a project that honors one of the human treasures that Nigeria has been blessed with; in the person of Chief Chika Okpala, MON, MFR, FTA, a.k.a. Chief Zebrudaya Okoroigwe Nwogbo, alias 4:30. A man of humility, sincerity and contentment. A relentless and disciplined artist, very easy to work and get along with. I am not just heaping accolades, I write from my experience and I have worked with quite a few artists. Having been fortunate to work with Chief Chika Okpala, and spend months under one roof with him, I can say with authority that Chief Okpala is an actor's actor, and a rare gem of a person.

At a young age and like many other Nigerians, I was an avid fan of the then number one drama series on televisions across Nigeria, West Africa, and beyond titled, "Masquerade" (or "New Masquerade" as it was later renamed). I remember how we cleared our schedules and endure long travel distances just to watch the TV-show on any black-and-white television we could find in the town or city we lived in as there were not many televisions available in those days. For the next several days, after the airing of the week's episode of the show, we commented and revisited the events that took place in the episode and entertained ourselves with repeated laughter as we awaited the next episode that would air the next week.

It was therefore, not unusual that when the trend of Nollywood movies went global, many of us hoped to see the veterans of the show, Masquerade starring in them. We expected to see more of the likes of Chief Zebrudaya Okoroigwe Nwogbo, alias 4:30 (Chika Okpala) in his no nonsense elderly demeanor delivering his unique rendition of the English grammar while addressing matters of the day; Jegede Shokoya, "the youngest millionaire" (Claude Eke) in an endless display of ebullient and flamboyant Yoruba lineament; Ovuleria (Lizzy Eveome) the sometimes patient but also assertive housewife who always had a way to humbly check the conservative standpoints of Chief Zebrudaya even as she accommodated his mannerisms; Clarus (Davies Offor) the crafty houseboy who always wanted to be the boss when his bosses (Chief Zebrudaya and the Madam Ovuleria) were away from home; Gringory Akabogu (James Iroha), in his Cross River/Akwa-Ibom houseboy accent would be clashing with co-houseboy, Clarus in one moment and would be conniving with him in the next moment; Apena (Christy Esien Igbokwe) the cantankerous and outspoken housewife of Chief Jegede Shokoya; Natty (Romanus Amuta), the ever so calm but needy and gluttonous family friend. There were other members of the cast such as Zakky (Tony Akposheri), Ramota (Veronica Njoku), and so on. The show was so popular that the catchy sound tracks of the series titled, "Eddie Kwansa" by legendary Peacock Guitar Band, became a kind of everlasting song cherished by even those who could not understand the Igbo lyrics. The performance of these actors and others who worked with them, transcended tribe, politics, religion, class, or status. These actors were the darling of many Nigerians and with others in similar TV shows such as, "Village Headmaster," "Cock Crow at Dawn," "Basi & Co," they entertained Nigerians and held the fort for decades as the contemporary theater, movie, and music entertainment industries that emerged and garnered high global ranking. Yet, there were no clear significant effort made to safeguard them as the national treasures and assets, which they were. We did not see them riding the wave of Nigeria's emerging prominence in global entertainment. They were not reaping the fruit of the entertainment industry that they helped build and held up for decades. Instead from time to time, we heard one sad news or the other about how one of these actors was either suffering from one illness or eventually dying in despair and want.

Sadly, the stories of these actors being neglected and not appreciated seemed known by the general public, yet no one seemed to do something about it, or at least, not enough seemed to have been done in that regard. The writer/creator of the series James Iroha (Gringory) cried out in a number of his last interviews about his abject condition, yet not much happened and he eventually died. Report has it that Claude Eke (Jegede) died of hypertension and diabetes. Davis Offor (Clarus) was reportedly blind for over ten years and lived in poverty. This trend has continued till present day and many veteran actors are ill and dying in abject poverty. Typical of Nigerian society, when these actors die, they are celebrated with eulogies, lavish parties, or even extravagant state burials. What about doing something to help them while they are alive?

It does not seem that any significant government effort has been invested in caring for these actors or even tried to protect their legacies. One would think it would be a good idea to obtain these tapes and remaster the content and circulate them to raise fund and value for these veteran actors but the report is that footage of these well-loved episodes that were broadcast by the government/state owned National Television Authority (NTA) were not saved or protected. Instead, while some of the tapes in which the episodes were recorded could not be found, most, if not all of the tapes found, have been erased by fresh recordings of other unrelated programs. The report out there is that the same fate befell the TV episodes of Chinua Achebe's "Things Fall Apart." One can only hope that this kind of regrettable practice in our government owned/run television stations have been corrected by current managers and that video content of our heritage is being protected henceforth.

Knowing the importance of safeguarding creative content, I thought that there would be a way to have these legendary actors express their talent through new creative content. It would also help in introducing these actors to the New/contemporary generation and perhaps help them earn some resources to help themselves and their situations in their veteran years. Incidentally, I did not find companies eager to invest in these veteran actors. Many entertainment or film making companies out there want the new popular A-list faces. It was simply a matter of profitable business decision for them to go with younger newer actors. It became obvious to me that we may have to simply do the little we can in any way to make these veteran actors relevant. It was in line with that thinking I created the "Cultures TV Series" which was adapted to accommodate the peculiar grammatical style for which Chief Chika Okpala has been known for. Incidentally, I was able to find an understanding ear in the person of my friend, Sir Felix Citor Nnorom, who teamed up with me to invite Chief Chika Okpala to the United States to shoot the series and play the role of "Chief Anabaraonye Akaepusionwa AAA." Sadly, we were unable to have the other masquerade cast members on board as most were then deceased and those surviving were not in the state to travel to the US for such an intense production.

Yet, we were convinced that if people could see Chief Chika Okpala out there performing, it would bring back to memory the talents and relevance of his veteran colleagues and by extension shed some light on the plight of other surviving veterans. Gladly, when we released parts of "Cultures" series it was a thing of joy to note that many out there still valued Chief Chika Okpala. In fact he was subsequently invited abroad by other diaspora organizations and even some companies in Nigeria have since shown interest in him and other veteran artists. Later part of the series remained unreleased.

While all renewed interest in any of these veterans is appreciated, it must be pointed out that the work is just beginning. I humbly urge the government and relevant organizations to be more involved in the lives of our veteran actors in a more consistent and significant way. They have to be treasured and valued for their contributions to the society and the entertainment industry. We must have a system and practice that ensures that veteran artists are appreciated when they retire or approach old age. They have to be cared for and provided with efficient healthcare while they are alive and in need of it. We must not wait for them to die before they are lavishly celebrated and remembered on the pages of newspapers, or become subjects of media headlines and breaking news.

It is along this line that I express my thanks and appreciation for the efforts of our brother, Chief Alex Iheke of Igbo Basics for this noble idea to have a book in the name of our treasured veteran, Chief Chika Okpala. Let us join to appreciate this creative treasure while we can and while he is still with us. So that when as is inevitable in life, he is no longer here with us, we will continue to remember him with smiles on our faces for the laughter and happiness he brought to our lives, and not with sadness and regret that he could have been treated better.

PART SIX

NOLLYWOOD, HIS VIEWS AND STATE OF THE NATION IN PERSPECTIVE

6.1 Nollywood: Challenges & Prospects

6.2 State of the Nation in Perspective

6.1 NOLLYWOOD: CHALLENGES & PROSPECTS??

In the world of entertainment, the Nigerian movie industry – Nollywood - is somehow younger than that of many frontline nations of the world such as the American Hollywood, created (1910), the Bollywood of India, developed in Mumbai (former Bombay) in 1930, Telemundo, founded in 1984 in the Latin American world, the Chinese film industry formally introduced in Shanghai in 1913 with "the Difficult Couple", shot 8 years after the very first Chinese film, Dingjun Mountain was made in 1905; the Cinema of Korea (Kpop) referring to the Korea movie industry founded (1945) and more advanced and now being referred to as the Hallyuwood in South Korea.

Nevertheless, Nollywood is rated the third largest movie industry, after Hollywood and Bollywood. "Even with the negative factors affecting the nation, a movie industry was created and went on to become one of the world's largest."

Contentproject.weebly.com reported. It is a common notion that the Nigeria movie industry – Nollywood began in 1992 with the epical Living In Bondage. Nevertheless, the history of Movie Industry in Nigeria is older than the 1990s AD. According to Britannica.com; Herbert

Ogunde was a pioneer in the field of Nigeria folk opera. He created the Ogunde Concert Party also known as the Ogunde Theater in 1945. It was the first theatre company of the nation; and due to his contributions to the creation of the Nigeria film industry, he is often hailed as the father of Nigerian theatre.

It is also known that after Ogunde, came others whose works laid the ground work for the advancement of the movie industry in the 1960s when the sweet breeze of Independence blew on the nation. As Contentprojectweebly.com affirmed; The creation of

Nollywood started in the 1960s. It was when the first Nollywood movies were being created by historical filmmakers such as Ola Balogun, Hubert Ogunde, Jab Adu, Moses Olayia and Eddie Ugboma. They are considered the first generation of Nigerian filmmakers. These pioneers started the Nigeria film industry in a country full of citizens that looked to Hollywood for their entertainment.

It should equally be stated that while Herbert Ogunde, Ola Balogun and other pioneers were holding sway in the western coast of Nigeria, Anyaogu Elekwachi Ukonu (Mazi Ukonu) – was rocking the American theater and movie world with his African sensational skills to book his place as one of the first indigenous African movie stars and film makers. He returned to Nigeria in the 1960s with his inimitable filmmaking prowess. Through the Eastern Nigeria Broadcast Corporation he played pioneering roles with viable footprints in the making of the movie industry in the land from the Eastern Coast of the Nation.

Before the coming of Living in Bondage movie, the late 1980s and early 1990s witnessed local movies across Igbo land and beyond such as "Ihe dina Okpuru Anyanwu, "Uwa ezuoke" etc. Most of the stars and producers of these local movies simply harmonized into the Nollywood as pioneer stars and producers. Chief Chika Okpala – Chief Zebrudaya confirmed this;

The New Masquerade as a phenomenon has everything to do with the evolution of Nollywood. It is a pioneer audio-visual entertainment that opened the doors to the benefits of comedy to Nigerian people by way of commercial enterprises in Nigeria. It was mobile on stage and available in audio and video tapes. I have been involved in so many Nollywood films that do not offend my conscience.

Besides, the New Masquerade, Wale Adenuga's Super Story and other sitcom soap operas, running on national and state television stations in Lagos and other zones, produced the artistes who flocked into Nollywood at its onset. This brought about a healthy situation where the array of more educated young professionals with interest to make their marks in the new industry were complementing the experience and exposure of the veterans in the field. Besides, there with funds, marketing and distribution outlets provided by the enterprising Igbo traders at Aba, Onitsha, Lagos and other parts of Nigeria. The nascent Nollywood was bound to explode into global reckoning in less than a decade of its existence.

As if in a hurry to catch up with the rest of the world, the budding industry began to mill out films of all genres weekly with the ease of well-fed poultry laying eggs. In due course, Nollywood became a hub of discovery of Nigeria's large army of highly talented actors and actresses gracing the unprecedented number of productions that has left Africa and the entire world stunned by the good, the bad and the ugly socio-cultural trends coming out of the African giant.

CHALLENGES & PROSPECTS

Well, the phenomenal surge of Nollywood into global reckoning in so short a time, was never without its intrinsic negativities. The ills are diverse, stirring lamentation, heard more vociferously from the elders and veterans of the industry. Chief (Mrs.) Lizzy Evueme, Ovularia of the New Masquerade in her candid appraisal of the industry, took quite a time to express her sadness and joy over Nollywood. She began on a happy note expressing profound gratitude to the facilitators; "The people who introduced Nollywood, who put it together and brought it out for us, did a great and wonderful work as they are still doing. I give a thumps up to some actors and actresses in the Nollywood. I can't mention them one by one, but there are some great artistes in the Nollywood."

Then on a sad and disappointing note, the octogenarian dame of the industry was quite specific on those she sees as the problems of Nollywood:

"My grudge against Nollywood is on some of the writers, some of the directors and some of the producers. When we were in the New Masquerade, we had code of conduct, we had code of dressing and we had a check on the kind of language we could speak on air. We had dos and don'ts, but this time, I don't know! Some dresses you see some of our actors and actresses wear and some of the language they speak, on air, to me, is appalling. There are things that are never done on air that we can see these days. I begin to ask myself, what are we trying to show the world? What people see, what the world sees, they think that is who we are, but I don't think it is who we are. We portray these things and think we are giving the best. We are Nigerians and those of us from this part, we are mostly Igbos. What we are showing is not our culture. It's not! What matters nowadays is worldly, worldly, and worldly, whatever you do to make money is okay. It shouldn't be like that. It is true, there are people who don't believe in God, but whether we believe in God or not, God is still God and God is still up there. Let us think of our culture, let us remember the fact that we are Nigerians. They say what is good for the geese is good for the gander, it is not all true! Some things could be good for the geese but not for the gander. Some things would be good for the Oyibo people, but surely not good for the black man. That is what I think about Nollywood. Some people are good, give me a script, I will read it and tell you whether I will do it or not, if it goes against what I believe, I wouldn't do it. It doesn't matter how much you offer me; I wouldn't do it. Because I have children, I have younger brothers and sisters. I would think, what would they learn from this thing I am doing? What is the lesson am teaching them? Nowadays, nobody thinks of that, all we think is how much?

Our people, my Ngwa people say; 'amaria uru esigharia isi.' Let us reconsider what we are sending out there, let us reconsider what we are giving to the younger generation. Look at the dance style that is reigning nowadays, it wasn't like that during our own days . . . "your time has gone, you enjoyed yourself when it was your time, please, let us live our lives . . ." they will say. But I am saying; it doesn't end there, after all these enjoyments, there is a tomorrow. E don finish for my mouth o!

Toeing Ovularia's line of summation on the ills of the Nollywood today, Leo-Spider Osuji, member of the Elders Forum at Enugu, comparing standards of today and yesterday in Nollywood said;

"Let me be honest, every generation has its greats and underlings, its high and low times. Some people would say during our time we had the best ever, ours were the best. But a time comes when these best times give way to new trends and go into oblivion. So, it is in the industry. Nevertheless, there are certain things we do which we are not supposed to be doing. For example, in the olden days, films taught morals, today, what do we present to the people to view? They call it glamour . . . I don't know what manner of lessons it teaches.

Although these things are coming down gradually, we need to jettison them.

I remember Zebrudaya refused to enter Nollywood at the early stage because he said they were more interested in rituals, portraying us as a people who are interested in killing people for rituals. Even up till now, give him a role where people are killed, he will not act it. Generally, anyway, there's improvement and Nollywood is moving, although we are not up to the standard of the Bollywood not to talk of the Hollywood. All in all, I will submit a case of mixed feelings on this."

In his view, Chika is quite positive and obviously impressed by the efforts of Nollywood National Executive Committee led by Emeka Rollas Ejezie. He noted that there has been a visible positive twist in upgrading the welfare of the artistes in the industry. He outlined some of these positive efforts of the present crop of the Nollywood Management Committee to include;

Their visible drive to advancing the course of proper artiste management, provision of insurance scheme for the registered members, intervening to secure proper and reasonable artiste fees for its members, securing government productions for the Nollywood industry.

Chief Okpala believes also that there is room for improvement and one sure way to this is by investing in training and retraining of players in the industry, professional management of storylines and ethical conduct of the artistes, producers and directors, as well as concentrating on constructive storylines indigenous to Nigeria and Africa, while securing partnership deals with auto-mobile industries, government ministries, parastatals/agencies, etc.

With this, Nollywood will be on the forward match to attaining the heights of the famous Hollywood industry of America. A Nollywood with a bright new dawn and a new set of values and viability that would guarantee the practitioners commensurate livelihood from their God-given talents and endeavour in the industry.

ROLL CALL

For the records, some of the living and dead veteran thespians who graced the Nollywood with their wealth of experience to give the nascent Industry a boost at its inception included; Chief Chika Okpala – Chief Zebrudaya; Chijoke Abagwe, Ojemba; Pete Edochie (Okonkwo Ebubedike of Things Fall Apart fame); Olu Jacobs and wife, Joke; Justus Esiri, of the New Village Headmaster fame; Jide Kosoko; Dan Enebeli, (Andrew); Zulu Adigwe, of the Basi & Co fame); Alex Usifo; Pete Eneh; Alex Adibe; Chiwetalu Agu; Sam loco Efe; David Ihesie; Dan Nkolagu; Nkem Owoh, (Osuoffia); Roy Denani; Major Okoro, (Old Major); and many others.

For the female greats, we have such names as; Lizzy Evueme (Ovularia); Madam Owoh; Patience Ozokwor, (Mama G); Rachel Oniga; Susan Obi; Vicky Madukife; and other radio and TV veterans across the country. From the music industry came some veteran music icons in our clime such as Onyeka Owenu; Nelly Uchendu; Jonel Cross; Ferdinand Ohans; Ifanyi Gbulie and wife, Lade; Camila Mbrekpe and remarkably, HRH Prof. Laz Ekwueme, the Igwe of Oko Kingdom in Orumba, Anambra state. They found Nollywood a refreshing platform to diversify and explore their acting skills.

For the younger generation, there were indeed stars from all regions of the country who were the very early casts of Nollywood. They became household names as they dazzled with such glowing glamour and grandeur that attested profoundly to the glory of Nigeria's enviable multi-tribal diversity. Some of these stars that readily come to mind include, indefatigable Kenneth Okonkwo, (Living in Bondage fame,) now a legal practitioner; Zack Orji; Kanayo O kanayo; Clems Ohamaeze; Bob manuel Udokwu; Keppy Ekpenyong; Emeka Ossai; Saint Obi; Gentle Jack; Charles Okafor, Ejike Asiegbu; Naths Eboh; John Okafor (Mr. Ibu); Charles Awurum; T. West; Kalu Ikeagwu; Desmond Elliot; Segun Arinze; Ifeanyi Duru; Muna Obiekwe; Mike Ezuruonye; Emeka Ani; Hank Anuku; Van Vicker; Ramsey Noah; Emeka Ike; Pat Attah; Nonso Eriobu; Stanley Okereke; Clemson Cornell Agbogidi etc.

The ladies are: Rita Edochie; Eucharia Aninonbi; Liz Benson; Susan Patrick; Ngozi Ezeonu, Ngozi Nwosu; Ngozi Nwaneto; Chinyere Wlifred; Franca Brown; Ndidi Obi (Nneka d' pretty Serpent); Hilda Dokubo; Sandra Achums; Shuan George; Alex Lopez; Nkiru Silvanus; Oge Okoye;

Genevive Nnaji; Omotola Jalade Ekhinde; Funke Akindele

(Jennifer); Kate Henshaw; Ini Edo; Rita Dominic; Stellar Damasus; Jennifer Eriobuna; Uche Osotule, Uche Jombo; Mercy Johnson; Chika Ike; Stephanie Okereke Linus; Chioma Chukwuka; and so many of others.

Note that this is just a random pick of names, by all means; it's not a comprehensive roll call of all pioneer Nollywood stars in Nigeria.

With this array of stars, the Nollywood was actually set to confront other frontline entertainment industries of the world. In the Nollywood firmament, more and more glamour and graceful thespians of the new age in the bourgeoning industry are emerging. This is as the quality of production has equally improved in consonance with the evolutionary trends in technology of the modern production tools and the psychology of the producers, directors and the thespians of the digital era.

6.2: HIS VIEWS ON THE NATION AND BIAFRA AGITATION

The run of things in the post-civil war Nigeria of today shows that the 30 months' bloody war failed woefully to bring about a true One Nigeria it was said to be fought for. The No Victor No Vanquished declaration at cease fire in 1970 was obviously, a fortuitous political statement made for cosmetic massaging of the vanquished Easterners while hoodwinking the incensed world from raking up war crime charges for the incalculable atrocities of the federal fighting forces at the battle fronts. Above all, the war neither answered the ethnic question nor corrected the foundational default of one Nigeria laid by our colonial lords. It never conquered the

Igbo spirit or stemmed the hate for the Igbo resilience and peregrination.

Regrettably, in well over sixty years of sovereignty of nationhood, Nigeria is in quandary, embattled and bayed all round by internal destabilizing factors. Boko Haram, ISWAP and ISIS in the Northeast; Cattle rustling and banditry in the Northwest, roving brigands of Fulani herdsmen and bandits launching guerilla spreading across the North Central down the Southern Territories -East and West of the Niger.

In the South-south region, the Niger-Delta militants, once upon a time, launched a dogged arms resistance against the Nation's military, launching destructive raids on oil installations in the area. The age-long neglect and collateral damages of the habitation and environment of the Niger Delta regions for the nation's common wealth and the iron-fist control of these resources and playing god with it to the detriment of the resource base was indeed, their reason for the run of violent dissensions in the Niger Delta region. They may appear ostensibly calm for now, but we know as Ndi Igbo would say; "oku dara ibube anughi anyu." Meaning; "a raging flame doused into ashes is only latent, and certainly not dead."

In the land-locked Igbo Southeast zone of Chika Okpala, the vociferous echoes and uprising of separatist regional movements since 1999 were rather peaking instead of mellowing. It was Movement for the Actualization of the Sovereign State of Biafra (MASSOB) led by Chief Ralph Uwazuruike then. Now it's the Indigenous People of Biafra (IPOB) led by Mazi Nnamdi Kanu.

In what looks like tacit fascination of the trend, a crop of Yoruba activists in the Southwest led by Sunday Adeyemo Igboho, came up with their own movement for actualization of the Oduduwa nation for the Yorubas.

It is a common knowledge that Chika Okpala's Igbo people of the Southeast were not particularly favored by President Buhari's eight year reign. The General had occasionally betrayed curious reflexes of acrimony with flips of unpresidential hate utterances and actions against the Igbo, which he described as a Dot Nation.

A typical example of his malevolent utterances against the young Biafran agitators that drew cyclones of global damnation and the ire of twitter runners that promptly shut down his account on June 2, 2021 is this; "Many of those misbehaving today are too young to be aware of the destruction and loss of lives that occurred during the Nigeria Civil war. Those of us in the field for 30 months will treat them in the language they understand."

The unabating attacks and mass killings of the hitherto nonviolent Biafran agitators in the Southeast, smack more of perpetuation of the extermination bid against the Igbos which in the main was the furtive and ultimate aim of the civil war declared ended more than half a century ago.

This has been a thing of great worry to many Nigerians at home and abroad. Sharing his thoughts and misgivings on this worrisome oppression and suppression of his Igbo tribal family in Nigeria, Chief Chika Okpala - the Great Zebrudaya Okoroigwe Nwogbo alias 4.30 said; O Yes! Mr. President are right that the young youth of boys and girls agitating agitation of Biafra are not see the ogbunigwe and are not hear the shelling machines sing; "kwafu-Kwafu-kwafu! Unu duum!!"

But today, dis young youth are suffering of the wicked fall out of that war with no end in sight. How are the Igbo young youth of boys and girls going to understand why. Even the chief okokorokoo are segregation and discrimination against them? Why the bad belle denial of federal amenities in Igbo land? Why are they denied national opportunities given to others in the land because of the civil war? And you are want dem to remain patriotic nde?

In fact, if we are to talk true and nothing but de true talk to shame oga devil, the question we are ask our self first be; how are we going to tell these Igbo young people to forget their dream for Biafra and accept to be called Nigerians? Let me ask it again, Forgetful; are it by every day by day deny of their Constitutional Rights and Freedom to live and do their buying and trading business? Is it by every daylily harassment of government security people who are come to occupy every kilometer of the highways in the East, extort moni, plus fire and kill as they like? Told me! How are we to convince them when in the open korokoro

political tugs... are set fire... where Igbos are live and do business in great number of Igwe madu in the very before of government security officers who are look the other way at any slightest provocation in the country.

Just told me, so that I, Chief Zebrudaya Okoroigwe Nwogbo alias 4.30 would know! What are the Federal Government does to the dem people of Miyetti Allah etc etc...?

They rape our daughters and slaughter our villagers, burn their houses even plus including slaughter of infants and babies like nama every daylily and government are keep their mouth sum, and look the other way.

How many of the nama people parambulating here and there killing people have they arrested?

How can we as their fathers explain to this young youth of people that FG are ban every Nigerian from carrying guns, but every day by day they are see these nama herders said to be fellow Nigerians carrying Ak-47 guns' perambulation their nama/cows in the streets and invasion farm lands.

Oya, hanlele to decode this irony where Government are choosing to kill those protesting and protecting their homesteads and proscribe them terrorists, while the roving killer nama men invading and opendentially burning down villages and towns, leashing mass death on their tracks are not branded terrorists? As a matter of fact, Government are told the victim communities if they want to survive they should accommodate and live in peace weda or wedant with their killers. Even when the media are expose the atrocities of this nama men on televisions, shout it on radio, television and newspapers what are government does? Given all these run of injustices, you are still expecting this Igbo young youths who we are deny in their schools, the history of the

war, what are bring the war, and the true consequences of the war not to agitate for a separate Nation which they can call their own and have peace for themselves and posterity? Ka Chineke mezie okwu!

Lending his voice to this too, Okonkwo Ebube dike of Things Fall Apart, Chief Pete Edochie said; I say I saw the war, I don't pray for a second experience again. Most of the people today angling for war never experienced it. You see, Ndi Igbo have suffered a lot, just that there's perseverance as an ingredient in the composition of every Igbo man. This is why we specialize in picking up the threads, you know! They burn our stalls; we pick up the threads and continue. I think it's about time we are given some peace, chasing us about like rats in this land will do no one any good."

Well, it's instructive to note here that if the "Operations Python Dance (Egwu Eke) 1 & 2" were meant to cow and dislodge the young agitators into abandoning their course, this has been largely counterproductive. Paradoxically, it has actually, hardened the young agitators into abandoning their non-violent preachments into launching a militant resistant wing named the Eastern Security Network (ESN). This is akin to UMKONTHO WESIWE - Spear of the Nation, launched in South Africa by the African National Congress (ANC), as its military wing. This was led by its youthful fiery anti-Apartheid fighter, late Chris Hani, in the hay days of the anti-apartheid struggle in the Rainbow land.

The supreme leader of the IPOB Mazi Nnamdi Kanu in sync with the rhythm of the federal Government's drumbeats of war against them simply became ruthless and relentless in his venoms and malevolent invectives against the person of Mr. President.

Akin to President Obama's regime gratifying the Americans with decisive ending of the fear of Osama Bin Ladi, Gen. Buhari's capturing of Mazi Kanu on June 4, 2021 from Kenya and rendering him into the country to face treason charges remains one of his Government's eternal achievements to the utmost delight of mostly his Fulani tribe's men. Therefore, expecting him to have obeyed Supreme Court orders and release Kanu in his reign was as akin as asking the Philistines of the old to release Sampson from their holding.

APPENDIX

THE NEW MASQUERADE STARS AT A GLANCE

CAST

CHIKA OKPALA - Chief Zebrudaya

JAMES IROHA - Gringory Akabogu

LIZZY EVOEME- Ovularia Urediya Nwogbo

DAVIS OFOR - Clarus Mgbojikwe

CLAUDE EKE - Prince (DR.) Jegede Shokoya

CHRISTY ESSIEN IGBOKWE - Akpenor

ROMANUS AMUTA - Natty

VERONICA NJOKU - Ramota

TONY AKPOSHERI - Zachy

ROY DE NANIE - Sergent Kpafu

IFEANYI GBULIE - Ikenga

CAMILLA MBEREKPE - Boma

CHINWE UGWU - Aforlene

JAMES AKWARI UDENSI IROHA, OON (1942– 2012)

Chief James Akwari Udensi Iroha, once in a heated conversation with a colleague pressing to know his family background hilariously exclaimed; "I am one of the several sons of my father! Anam anu ihe!" This was to shut off the inquisitive peer, while letting him know he was never a lone child, but one born into the offspring bounteous family of Mazi Akwari Iroha of Amaba, Amokwe Item, in Bende LG of Abia state.

As already stated, he was born on the 12th of October 1942, and had his early education in Bukuru, Jos, of the old Northern region, but now Plateatu State. His secondary education was in Calabar, capital city of the present Cross River State of Nigeria. This is where he learnt to speak his impeccable Efik and the character traits of a typical Efik houseboy he depicted in his role in the new masquerade he created and produced. He equally spoke Hausa, which he picked up as toddler growing up in Jos, French and of course, English his lingua Franca.

For his university education, Iroha passed through the prestigious University of Ibadan and obtained a diploma certificate in Theatre Arts, and a Bachelor of Science Degree in Mass Communication.

He joined the Eastern Broadcasting Service (ENBS) in Enugu in 1967 as TV programme producer. Along the line of service, he rose to the rank of Director TV and Deputy Director General.

Attesting to how he came about the creation of the phenomenal drama series, the Masquerade, Iroha enthused;

"Just after the Biafra war ended, people had no business or reason to smile, let alone laugh. Then, if one hadn't lost a mother, then it must be the father, or an uncle or even a twin sister. At that point, I had this emotional burden to put a smile back on people's faces again. This was how the divine inspiration that gave birth to the MASQUERADE

(Satirical TV Drama) came to me. First, it started off on stage with live audience, and then moved on to radio and later TV as a local content programme. And finanlly, it became a national programme on the Nigeria Television Authority (NTA) and across Africa. Ever since then, I have been referred to be as one of Nigeria's most hilarious comedians. Anam anu ihe! Did I mention I was the Premier Director of Imo state Council of Arts and Culture, (ISCAC)? Yes, I was from 1980 – 1982.

Well, he also forgot to mention that he led the Masquerade team to the FESTAC show in 1977, and joined the Imo Broadcasting Service to help boost and nurture the station. Again, he was nationally recognized by his nation, Nigeria as one of the early recepients of the national honours of the Officer of the Order of the Niger (OON)

James Akwari Udensi Iroha was a versatile human memorabilia of the theatre, a superlative content creator in broadcasting. He indeed, left indelible footprints and infinite honour no money can buy. The hilarious and timorous Gringori Akabogu of Ikot 4 died at age 69 on 28 February 2012.

CHIEF MRS. LIZZY EVOEME – OVULARIA

Chief Lizzy Evoeme was popularly known as Misisim Ovularia Urediya Nwogbo alias G4. She was born in January1942 to a seafaring father based in the old Calabar of the old Eastern Region, but now the capital city of Cross River State. She is a native of Akabo in Ikeduru Local Government of Imo State by birth, but married to Mr. Israel Erondu Evoeme of Umuaba village in Obioma Ngwa, Osisioma Local Government of Abia state.

Before hitting lime light with the New Masquerade in the late 1970s, she joined as the third, in the series of wives of the lead actor, Chief Zebrudaya. Elizabeth had earlier acted with other cast in a small theatre group.

DAVIS AKALIRO OFFOR – CLARUS MGBOJIKWE

Davis Offor aka Clarus Mgbojikwe was born April 6, 1942 at Bende town of the old Bende LG of Abia State. He began his early education in Methodist Central Primary School, Bende town in 1947; two years after, in 1949, a teacher by name Mr. Okorie Kanu took him as a houseboy. He went with him on transfer in 1950 to Methodist Primary School, Umuhu, Abam, now Umuhu Ezechi. That same year (1950), the teacher was transferred again to Bende to teach at the Methodist Primary School, Lohum, where he continued with his education from 1950 - 1953. Since Methodist Primary School did not have primary six, he had to switch to St. Joseph Catholic Primary School, Bende in 1954 to enable him to sit for his First School Leaving Certificate exam. It is important to note that his houseboy experience with his school teacher came handy in playing his role years later in the New Masquerade - as acting big man. Obtaining his School Leaving Certificate in St Joseph in 1954, he proceeded to Holy Ghost College, Owerri for his secondary school from 1956 to 1960, where he obtained the West African School Certificate (WASC). He joined the accounts department of Post and

Telecommunication in Enugu the following year, 1961; and later trained/served as a Litigation Officer in the Ministry of Justice, Lagos. While in Lagos, there was a plan for him to travel to England in May, 1966, unfortunately, the January 15, 1966 coup truncated the plan. In his tenacious hope that the plans would still materialize, Davis stayed back in Lagos and waited while events unfolded for the worse.

Later that same year, on July 29, to be precise, the counter coup by northern officers occurred and deepened the bloody crisis that rocked the country. It became obvious to Davis that the England travel would not happen and his hope for it had become forlorn. He then attempted to return to the East but the road was closed. The high Sea was the only option, so he had to join others to travel by sea from Lagos to Port Harcourt as Southeasterners mobilized for the civil war.

At the end of the war, Davis returned to Enugu where he came in contact with James Iroha at the Enugu Writers Workshop, who was then engaged in part-time drama shows/ productions. He participated in the dramas James produced for the Eastern Nigeria Broadcasting Corporation (ENBC). This is how Davis Offor found his way into broadcasting; and explored comedy - his natural trait. “I have been a comedian right from my childhood, comedy is in my blood. I inherited it from my parents . . .”, Davis attested.

With the creation of states in 1976, he relocated to new Imo State and joined Mazi Ukonu in the NTA, Aba to continue with the

Masquerade drama series.

He was later to join the NTA services as Trainee Producer in 1977, on Grade Level 08. Though he left NTA at some point, Davis worked his way back into the services of the NTA between 1985/86 as a contract staff and rose to middle management, but was, however, rationalized out of the system in 1994 due to his visual impairment. He is an ordained reverend minister of the Aetherus Churches Worldwide and was married to Juliet Mecha, with five children before their divorce in 2010. Davis lost his sight to glaucoma in 1990, but has implicit faith that God will someday restore his sight for him to see the world once again before his death.

CLAUDE EKE – PRINCE JEGEDE SHOKOYA

I, Honourable Prince Dr. Jegede Shokoya, son of the soil, and the great grandson of the Idi of Idi Araba and by the grace of God, the only young millionaire in the whole universe . . . tori Olonwu! This was the typical self-conceiting introduction many of us watching the New Masquerade heard from this Yoruba Character named Jegede Shokoya. Little did we know that he was a typical Igbo man! In short, from Mbaise in Imo State and his real name was Claude Eke! Indeed, Eke was gorgeous to watch displaying his peacock mannerism of a true Yoruba prince in his flowing Agbada and folded cap to match. He was indeed, the most loquacious and gregarious in the pack of the superlative talents that made the new Masquerade the most endearing of all sitcoms to hit the nation from the Eastern Coast of Nigeria. He depicted to the fullest the typical idiosyncrasies of an ebullient and elitist man of Western Nigeria. He was matchless in his role, quite consistent and loyal to the Masquerade project till he died in November 11, 2002.

CHRISTY ESSIEN IGBOKWE (MFR) [1960-2011] - AKPENOR

Christy Uduak Essien Igbokwe, Member of the Federal Republic

(MFR), ranked as one of the most versatile and multilingual female singers in Nigeria of her time, she sang in Ibibio/Efik, her native dialect, Igbo, her husband's language, Yoruba, where she lived, Hausa, and of course, English languages.

She was a native of Okat, Onna, now in Akwa Ibom State. She lost her mother early and was brought to live with a good friend of her mother at Aba. It was this foster mother (name unknown) that discovered Christy's singing talent and encouraged her. She was said to have bought Christy a fairly used cassette tape recorder to be recording her songs. It seems Christy paid more attention to music than Acting.

Nevertheless, she cut her teeth in acting with the New Masquerade on television. She played the role of Akpenor, the cantankerous wife of the egoistic Yoruba man, Prince Jegede Shokoya. Her performance of this role in the New Masquerade launched her into national fame before her music. Christy was said to have landed herself the role of Akpenor after she was said to have assisted a cast member get his role right during one of their rehearsals of the drama show. Ndaa Paul Akalonu was part of her music success as a producer.

Christy rose to become the first female President of the Performing Musicians Association of Nigeria (PMAN) in 1996. Christy married Edwin Igbokwe when she was barely 19 years. She remained a faithful wife and responsible superstar mother to her four sons and family till 30th June, 2011, when she passed on in Lagos before her 51st birthday.

ROMANUS AMUTA – NATTY (1943 – 2022)

Born 1943, Romanus Amuta, who played the role Natty Okosisi, was one of those pioneer casts of the Masquerade before it mutated to the New Masquerade. Amuta was from Ukana in Udi Local Government Area of Enugu State. He joined the crew at Aba to complete the circle of pioneer casts of the Masquerade to drive and sustain the sitcom at NTA, Aba in 1977. His lanky and hungry visage, his unique way of using his body language to communicate comically, his unstrained gluttony at the sight of food, made Romanus very apt for the role. He never said no to an invitation to join the table. He had a knack for arriving at auspicious moments when food is served in Chief Zubrudaya's house and would make straight to the table without washing his hands. On many occasions, Madam Ovularia would insist he should and go wash his hands before joining the eating. Natty will comically roll up his sleeves and even his trousers, wash his hands to his elbows, adjusting and salivating visibly in sheer rapaciousness. He was so good at his role that his name - Naatty and his alias Commissioner-for-longerthroat' became synonymous with greedy children in real life. Romanus sustained his role without replacement in the Masquerade till it changed to New Masquerade, despite the exit of many pioneer actors and the entrance of new casts. He battled with hardship and ailments and passed on February 10, 2022, at age 79 in a Lagos hospital.

VERONICA NJOKU – RAMOTA

Vero Njoku was one of those ex-staff of NTA who chose to resign and join the independent production world. She was the replacement of Christy Essien Igbokwe – Akpenor as wife of the loquacious Jegede Shokoya in the new Masquerade family. Vero was equally multilingual and very good in the role. Not many new she

was Igbo and not Yoruba. She was even more cantankerous than Akpenor and matched Jegede fire for fire. She was by all means a dame of the movie industry. Painfully, too Vero passed on in March 2017.

TONY AKPOSHERE – ZACHY

Tony Akposhere aka ZACHY, the Warri born actor/producer, was equally another of Chika's man Friday in the New Masquerade crew. Tony was a staff member of the NTA until 1998 when he, Vero Njoku (Ramota) and some others resigned with Chika to join the acting world. This was as a result of the draconian rule imposed on NTA staff members not to partake in external productions, advertising and even doing MC jobs. Many talented staff members, most popular of them all being Chika Okpala, the great Zebrudaya opted to leave the services of the NTA and serve as independent performers, producers and directors. Tony Akposhere was a production officer, but when he joined the new Masquerade crew, he became the production manager and doubled sometimes as director. A new role in which he was cast as Zaccheaus, which Jegede Shokoya relished calling Zakewus, (Zachy for short) was created and he played it with vive, making a huge success of it. He had a witty knack for releasing unique pidgin slangs that caught the fancy of pidgin English speakers. It was from Zachy we heard such slang as Kwoza for money, kack down for sitting down, paa-cool, for calm down or just relax, etc. Akposhere is a tireless vivacious person, lively, genial and a guru of Nollywood, both in acting, directing and producing films.

ROY DE NANI – SERGEANT KPAFU

Roy De Nani ranks as one of the popular faces of Nollywood today. He acted mostly in epic movies as a community elder and leader. He is one of those later day casts who tried to keep the New Masquerade going the extra distance before it went off air. Roy acted Sergeant and presented the ugly foibles of the police in the society. Sergeant Kpafu hardly made success of any case/arrest, but constantly insist they are on top of it as he plots to exploit Chief Zebrudaya and Prince Dr. Jegede Shokoya. Roy worked and retired from the railways in Enugu. He is a member of the Nollywood Elders Forum in Enugu.

IFEANYI GBULIE - IKENGA

Ifeanyi Gbulie is one of the old names in the entertainment Industry and broadcasting. Old in the act which he started young like Chika, Gbulie also ventured into the music world with an enchanting popular song entitled "Dis kind of woman" in which he did a duet with his Cameroonian born wife, Lade Gbulie. The song was a love sonnet and evergreen. His role in the later years of the New Masquerade was IKENGA, the affluent Ide ji obodo. The name stuck with him and even while he was one of the pioneer giants of Nollywood, versatile Ifeanyi acted any role from the rich affluent Ikenga to a motor park tout and delivered seamlessly. Painfully, hardship and ailments, including stroke took him.

CAMILLA MBREKPE – BOMA

The Uguta born thespian is equally one of the old stars of the industry. Camilla is a singer and songwriter with an Album to her credit. She featured in TV drama productions both at NTA, Enugu and the then Anambra TV Channel 50, long before the coming of Nollywood which she naturally dovetailed into. She also hit popularity as one of the later day casts of the New Masquerade, playing effectively the role of Boma, the educated niece of Chief Zebrudaya. She had become a great attraction to Prince Jegede Shokoya who was making passes; but Ramota would not stomach it.

Abia State of Nigeria Honours Zebrudaya @ 75

Zebrudaya @ 75; "Celebrate me while I am alive"

2025; Honor to whom honor is due as Abia State Government Celebrates Chief Chika Okpala aka Zebrudaya @ 75

"Dr. Alex Oti, has gone to brought the fish out of the water, to show you people, ndem" as Abia State Government celebrates Zebrudaya @ 75

ZEBRUDAYA AT 75

At 73, a zoom birthday celebration was organized by friends of Zebrudaya. ZB wished that his birthday when he turns 75 could be celebrated in person. And so it happened that a group of friends set out to organize Zebrudaya @ 75, intended to take place at a stipulated venue, but the group came short most events in life when based on pecuniary interest.

Events in life when based on love and labor of love succeeds. When such events are grounded on integrity and backed by power of the state, turns a resolution into successful celebration, and so it was that when the idea of Zebrudaya @75, connected with the commissioner of Culture, tourism and Creative economy of Abia

State, the event turned very successful. Abia State Government stepped up to fill the gap and celebrate Chief Chika Okpala aka Zebrudaya, a man Abia State adapted as their own, though he hails from Nnobi in Anambra State.

In a meeting at Zodiac Studios in Abakpa Nike, Enugu State on Sunday, March 2, 2025 Chief Chika Okpala in blessing the kola nut, prayed on "what we can do to change our attitude towards the living and the dead".

According to ZB's prayer, to change our attitude, we want to change the system to honor people when they are alive, not when they have died. That your loved one who is doing well and you think that you have done well by bringing all these things, does the family know you? The person who knows you is the man or woman you are burying, so we pray to God to help us to change the system.

"I emphasize that, the day we buried Ovularia, the Commissioner for Arts and Culture who came to represent the Governor, emphasized what his boss told him "that it is better to honor the people you cherished and their loved ones when they are alive, not when they have died. Whatever gift you want to give to him, give it to him when he is alive, whatever prayers you want to make for him, give it to him when they are alive, and when he sees how people love him, he will cease to die, he will say God, how can I abandon these people, my young ones and die? Please extend my life, that's all we are saying". We are trying, it is not easy. What we are doing is not a child's play. It is a revolution to say let's honor our loved ones when they are alive, not when they die. What we are saying is that those who love you should cherish you when you are alive not when you die, they carry one cow, all the beer come.

People wey know you, when you are celebrating your birthday, they pray for you asking God to keep you alive. Give you more health, more wealth. This envisioned practice is similar to the concept embedded in the Ezumezu Igbere cultural celebration of Igbere people, held every three years.

Ezumezu Igbere is an illustrious triennial homecoming event of Igbere people and friends of Igbere, celebrated from the third week of December to New Year's Day. The 2-day event mainly takes place on December 26th and 27th. Interdenominational Church service on Christmas day December 25, is purely a prelude to Ezumezu which for now takes place at Igbere Secondary School field. Primary activities at Ezumezu include, handing over of completed projects as previously promised by the retiring Age Grade. Other projects undertaken by various individuals and community organizations, national and international are acknowledged and received by the town as presented through Igbere Welfare Union IWU (the Governing Authority in Igbere). The other major activity is "Izara-afa (taking a name) by the youngest Age Grade such as Umu-Ebiri II, in the year 2023. Highlight of the activity at Ezumezu is the issuance of Certificate to individual members of the retiring Age Grade. The town also recognizes and welcomes the accomplishments of various individuals and community organizations.

After receiving certificates of Age Grade Retirement as presented by the Igbere Clan Council of NdiEze (composed by the 13 Kings of Igbere Autonomous Communities), individuals have options for private celebrations or receptions in which friends and families congratulate and celebrate the retiree with gifts and tributes. *It is fast becoming a cliché that what you will do for me when I am dead, do it now that I am still alive. If you plan to buy a cow and celebrate when I die, buy it now so that I can partake in the celebration of me.* Igbere is a town in Bende LGA of Abia State Nigeria.

ZB prayed God to bless this noble endeavor and objective for his 75th birthday Celebration. "Make it work, make it work, provide for us to move about, we will go places, give us health, give us life". IJN.

A huge Celebration at Banquet Hall, Government House, Umuahia, Abia State

After playing the theme song of New Masquerade 'Edie-Kwanzaa'.

Prayers were made for the departed members of the drama team and some minutes' silence was observed.

Referencing transcripts of the event, Chief Chika Okpala said he will form a Trust Fund to take care of his colleagues that are suffering. A Book "Chief Zebrudaya A Journey on Stage" written by Chief Chika Okpala was launched and the Governor of Abia

State bought 100 copies. The celebrant's cake was cut alongside with Actors Guild Elders Enugu, the Governor, His Wife, Deputy and other Distinguished guests including Rev. Davis Ofor aka Clarus. Paulson Kalu performed on Stage. Highlights of old New Masquerade drama were shown.

Governor Otti addressed the audience saying MON without EY but said, by the time you leave here today, you will have the EY and of course your real wife Mrs. Okpala thank you so much, you are not Mrs. Okoroigwe Nwogbo, Mrs. Okoroigwe was Ovularia who we have lost.

The Governor thanked the people; "distinguished ladies and gentlemen of the press, let me thank you for joining us to celebrate this great Icon, to celebrate a man that made a mark in his early days, pretending to be an old man. He needs to tell us what he used to whiten his hair and beards because as far back as the 70s, he was looking like a very old man and today you know how many years down the line he has just managed to turn 75 so he is still a very young man at least relative to Davis Ofor, Clarus Mgbojikwe at Ndi Olumbe who spoke so well, thank you very much sir. I will start with you, the comment about Chief Zebrudaya coming from Anambra".

Continuing, the Governor stated further, "I am just getting to know he came from Anambra. Our Government cares very little about where he comes from but remember that what you have today as Nollywood started in Aba, Pound Road, infact as at the time our movies were produced it was marketed from Pound Road and then Nnamdi Azikiwe, then to Upper Iweka, Onitsha but today, we have lost most of those things".

Persuaded to evaluate his observation about the ZB @ 75 Birthday Celebration, Chief Chika Okpala reluctantly proffered the following;

From the desk of Chief Zebrudaya Alias 4:30 - Amb. Chief Chika Okpala, mon, mfr, fta I am feel very odd to give account and score myself on the birthday celebration which was magnanimously and elaborately hosted by Abia State Government under Dr. Alex Otti OFR. The amiable Governor of Abia State at banquet hall, Government House Umuahia, Abia State.

"I am therefore presume it are celebrants over reach for me to score myself'. However, to make impute to what the them people who was attended the ceremony may say. The idea of celebrating my 75" birthday Anniversary was proceed to mind when Hon. Matthew C. Ekwuruibe, MCPN, MNCS, Honourable Commissioner of Arts, Culture and Creative Economy, Abia State gave a heart penetration address from Dr. Alex Otti, OFR The Executive Governor of Abia State at the funeral/ burial ceremony of my Revered Colleague Mrs. Elizabeth Nwanediya Evoeme who played the role of Mrsm Ovularia Urediya Nwogbo Alias G4 of French Language spokage creditably "RESKESE" "1 MEAN OF ...." in a sit-com series that ran for over two decades on NTA National Network. The NTA NEW MASQUERADE created by James Iroha, OON.

The funeral/ burial address was penetration my mind deep down. The key note was an appeal by Dr. Alex Otti OFR to celebrate our loved ones especially those who have impacted society when they are alive.

Having accepted the philosophy of Dr. Alex Otti OFR The Executive Governor of Abia State Nigeria, I mentioned it to friends and hinted about my 75' birthday celebration coming up on June 10, 2025 and my intention to give a percentage of gifts I may receive to vulnerable Artistes, colleagues in Actors Guild of Nigeria especially in the Elders forum and my mentors who made me who I am today in the Acting Industry. Most of them still alive are retired and some very sick.

I do not intend, acknowledging those who answered my call for support in my birthday celebration but permit me to acknowledge a couple I have never met one on one: Chigbo Okwudili Chukwu and Chigbo Nkeiruka Chinyere. They were the first to surprise me with a handsome gift.

To all those who contributed in different ways to the success of ZB @ 75 Birthday Celebrations especially the Government and the people of Abia State under Dr. Alex Chioma Otti OFR may the Almighty God bless you million fold. Amen..

Ka Chineke mezie okwu.

Goodwill Messages.

Goodwill messages were received by Chief Zebrudaya including one from Bishop Martin Uzoukwu, the Catholic Bishop of Minna Niger State see letter bellow.

CATHOLIC DIOCESE OF MINNA

Tel: +234-66-221239 *Residence*
Tel: +234-66-221046 *Office*
Mobile: +234-8037003784
E-mail: *bpmiuzoukwu@yahoo.com*

P. O. Box 33,
Minna.
Niger State, Nigeria.
bpmiuzoukwu@gmail.com

JUNE 9, 2025

TO: CHIEF CHIKA CHUKWUNONSO OKPALA

A.k.a Chief Zebrudaya Okoro Igwe Nwogbo: Alias 4:30

Through: BASIC ALEX IHIKE

U.S.A

CONGRATULATORY MESSAGE FROM THE CATHOLIC DIOCESE OF MINNA

On behalf of Most Rev Luka Sylvester Gopep, Auxiliary Bishop of Minna Diocese, the Priests, Religious and Lay Faithful of the Catholic Diocese of Minna, as well as the prayerful good wishes of the Missionaries of Divine Mercy Congregation (MDM), the Missionary Sisters of Saint Faustina (MSSF) and all the Lovers/Devotees of the Divine Mercy Devotion in Nigeria, I rejoice with you **CHIEF CHIKA CHUKWUNONSO OKPALA** on your 75TH birthday celebration.

It has pleased the Lord Jesus Christ the Divine Mercy Incarnate to enable CHIEF CHIKA CHUKWUNONSO OKPALA to mark/celebrate his 75th birthday. On a day like this, we give thanks to God the giver of life, health and the grace to live a life worthy of celebration. This is why it gladdens the heart of your family, friends, well-wishers and your children to gather to celebrate your goodness, your dedication, your love and service to humanity. Over the years, millions of Nigerians have watched your dramatic content on their Tv screen which was educative to the old and the young. The brilliant use of your unique language and spontaneous response to situation brings joy and laughter to your audience. The quiddity of your impart cannot be over emphasized. Thus, the Government of Abia State celebrates you. It is therefore our prayer that the Lord Jesus continue to keep you longer on earth for humanity to enjoy more of your goodness.

On an occasion of this magnitude, the joy, gratitude, and thankfulness in your heart towards God knows no bound and may this joy continue to keep you healthy, lively, faithful, dedicated and loving to humanity. The greatest gift and assurance I have for you is prayer that God will continue to bless you, your family and all who will attend the occasion with resounding success, safe journey to and fro and a good weather for the celebration.
Lastly, I would have loved to be present to celebrate with you, but I am bereaved over the demise of one of my spiritual sons Late Rev Fr James Omeh whom I just buried few days ago. Also, the natural disaster of flooding which happened few weeks ago in Mokwa, Niger State; a part of my Diocese, affected my people too. Therefore, I have to stay back to console my people and pray with them. Thanks for the understanding.

Congratulations to you **CHIEF CHIKA CHUKWUNONSO OKPALA** and May God bless you.

Yours sincerely in Jesus Christ and Mama Mary,

9/6/25

Most Rev. Dr. Martin Igwe Uzoukwu
Catholic Bishop of Minna
Jesus, Mary I Trust in You
Ambassador for Divine Mercy

Dr. Tony Aposheri aka Zaki who was youngest member of the cast, also sent a goodwill message.

Hon. Judge Oliver Mbamara chimed in from USA describing ZB as a humble man with good heart, he blends with both old and young alike. Chief Chika Okpala, ZB is a value the country has, that has not been truly appreciated. We praise western celebrities and actors more than we recognize our own. We have to praise our own and give value to whom value and honor is due. We thank God for keeping him alive today. It is only by the grace of God. God's hand is manifesting in him and we pray that he lives longer, that he continues to imbibe us with his love, charisma, charm, his entertainment and may God continue to give him happiness, even as he ages. Let him age with grace, let him age with health, happiness and joy and enjoy the fruits of the labor that he has planted all his life.

Obi Chika Okpala aka Zebrudaya, at his country home in Nnobi

Iconic Stage at Nnob, an off shore extension of Zodiac Brains Studio

CONCLUSION

This book is written about Chief Chika Okpala; The Man & Legend of New Masquerade Chief ZEBRUDAYA Okoroigwe Nwogbo Alias 4:30 so that the reader or whoever reads it will learn something about the life and times of Chika Okpala. He is endowed with the gift of gab.
Comedy, satire and laughter are good.. for the soul and is a good way to survive the effects of bad leadership and government policies in African setting.

Chika Chukwunonso Okpala is a natural born comedian with a unique twist of language as he set out from childhood, education, living and surviving through the Nigeria/Biafra civil war set out to bring joy to the faces of many in the face of adversity.

Chika set out to serve humanity even when he was considered not matured enough to serve in the Army during the war, he ended up serving by playing a vital role that gave hope and brought tears of joy to the faces of those who served in the war fronts.

Chika lives till date, a dignified life and did great works of service to generations, then, now and future generations to show his knowledge, and wisdom, that everyone would learn the value of comedy and satire as effective tools of communication to soften the often harshness of even the most ridiculous acts of bad governance. Since 1950s till date comedy has been used by ZB. Through his work, both governors and the governed are able to laugh humorously at idiosyncrasies without quarreling amongst themselves or taking their frustrations at the messenger.

Zebrudaya stands out as a legend who transcended through

generations with his unique language that new generations try to imitate. We wonder what angle AI (Artificial Intelligence) would follow to teach the ZB Chronicles to future generations.

In conversation with late Ovularia who played the role of ZB's TV wife in the New Masquerade, Lizzy Evoeme, Ovuleria pleaded to all who loved her and humanity to please assist ZB at his hour of need to fulfill his hearts desires which is to be fair and just to all, especially his fellow thespians and more so the ones in need of welfare. Chief Zebrudaya requested that the name New Mask Foundation for Artistes be changed to Chika Okpala Foundation for Artistes to encapsulate the entirety of his being, a man of honor and integrity.

The name Chika Chukwuunonso Okpala translated stands for Chika= God is Supreme, Chukwunonso, God is Near or is present, Okpala = first born.

EPILOGUE

If I would quote my children's exclamation when I first took them to Nnobi my home town, precisely to my house in my village, Ifite Ogbea-Diji, Ebenesi Nnobi in Idemili South Local Government Area of Anambra State, Nigeria; when I asked my first daughter and the eldest of my three children, Adaora who was ten: "What was the meaning of surprise, surprise, surprise? Why the exclamation: Surprise! Surprise!! Surprise!!?"

The three children burst into a wild laughter, so much that I insisted to know why the exclamation and the wild laughter that embarrassed their mother as well.

So picking up courage, Adaora said to her mother and I, "Mummy, so Daddy has this beautiful house at home and both of you never brought us to Nnobi our home town? Can you imagine all Christmas, New Year, and Easter holidays we spent at Aba and Enugu? Oh! Mummy, you and Daddy have not been fair to us." Then my wife told them that she was surprised too, adding that "Daddy has been saying he wants to build a house for us if his father allots a piece of land to him." "Your Daddy has eleven siblings; nine boys and two girls. So there was a need for our own house. Before now, we were squatting in his father's three-bedroom and parlor bungalow with his siblings who are also married with children," she said.

We all laughed it over, as Adaora hugged me for so long with filial affection.

As I opened the doors to the furnished rooms, the children jumped onto the beds in excitement, feeling so much at home.

So when Alexander N. Iheke, the author of "The Man and Legend of New Masquerade Chief Zebrudaya Okorigwe Nwogbo Alias 4:30" approached me, the book's co-author regarding the book's joint writing and publishing, we reached the following attached agreement binding the business, specifying: author, co-author, and publisher as well as distribution and marketing of the book.

Like my children, I shouted, "Surprise! Surprise!! Surprise!!!" And Alexander was both excited and surprised, asking what the surprise was about. I said, "Opiegbe," as he was fondly called, "I never knew that my foolishness, 'behaviourlarry' attitude on live stage, radio, television, and film would someday translate to attracting a book published for posterity.

Thank you for finding me worthy. Same gratitude goes to my producer, the late James Akwari Iroha, OON.

I once more join my children during their first visit to the village to shout: "Surprise! Surprise!! Surprise!!!"

Chief Chika Okpala, MFR, MON, FTA

REFERENCES

Faruk, U. (2011). *The victor and the vanquished of the Nigeria civil war.* Zaria: Nigeria, Ahmadu Bello University Press Limited.

Holy Bible – The King James Version retrieved KJV

Isaacson, W. (1999, Dec 31). Who mattered and why. *American Time Magazine*, 154(27), 18

Ladele, O. *et al.* (1979). *History of the NBC.* Ibadan: University Press.

National Broadcasting Commission (2012). *NBC Code* (5th Edition). Abuja Nigeria: National Broadcasting Commission

Nkama, O. (2013, March 05). *Ojukwu challenge of Biafra – A radio Documentary on the life and times of Dim Chukwuemeka Ojukwu* [Radio broadcast]. Radio Nigeria Network Service.

Nkama, O. (2021) *Akanu Ibiam: Eternal legacies of the royal statesman.* Enugu Nigeria: Nkamenia Africa Productions.

Nkama, O. (2022). *Broadcast journalists perception of National Broadcasting Commission's functions as a regulatory agency of Nigeria's broadcasting industry* [PG Research Study, Enugu State University of Technology (ESUT)].

Ogbankwa, D. (2023, June 01). *The Golden Days of the Nigerian Television Authority, (NTA).* https://frontiernewsng.com/the-golden-days-of-nigerian-television-authority/

www.allafric.com

www.Britannica.com

www.contentproject.weebly.com

www.Igbobasics.com

www.ingramcontent.com/pod-product-compliance
Lightning Source LLC
LaVergne TN
LVHW010857110826
845149LV00005B/1411

* 9 7 8 0 9 8 4 4 6 6 6 5 8 *